Forever
and a Day

Bob + Yvonne,

Enjoy

Robert Boeke

Rita Boeke

ISBN: 0-578-01429-7

EAN13: 9780578014296

LCCN: 2009925558

Visit www.booksurge.com to order additional copies.

Forever and a Day

An Invitation to Create
a Marriage that Lasts a Lifetime

Robert Boeke
&
Rita Boeke

We dedicate this work to our parents:

Edmund *and* **Margaret Fiely**

&

Victor *and* **Luella Boeke**

They taught us to love forever and a day.

ACKNOWLEDGEMENTS

Many people have played an important role in our journey and contributed to the experiences that made it possible for us to even think about writing a book. Thanks to the many people—couples, priests, and singles—who encouraged us when they said "If you ever write a book, we'll buy it!" Unending thanks to our great friend, Fr. Tom Burr, who walked much of our journey with us.

Thank you to Tom Widner, S.J., who was the first to read the manuscript and convince us that it was worth the effort to get it published. Thanks to Cindy Obringer who put up with our efforts to write while we were traveling together and for cheering us on as we wrote.

Thank you to Jeff and Kathy Wilhite, who read the manuscript and "tried it out," for encouraging us to keep working until it was finished. Special thanks for Kathy's multiple readings, insightful comments and corrections of our clumsy writing. The manuscript is better for her help. A simple thank you is not enough.

Our thanks to Katie and Bill Morris who generously allowed us to use their home to write while they honeymooned.

The book could not have been completed without the generosity of Michael and Stacey Boeke, who designed the cover and brainstormed marketing ideas, and Matthew Boeke for computer assistance. They were our biggest cheerleaders and number one fans. Thanks from the bottom of our hearts—we owe you big time.

Finally, we must thank our children—Daniel, Maria, Michael and Matthew. While we have tried to keep it our story in the telling, it would not be our story without them. Our story is enriched by Rhonda, Mike and Stacey, the spouses of our children. Together, they challenged us to begin writing, supported us along the way and eagerly read the manuscript even when they learned "too much information" about their parents. To each of you, we are forever grateful.

CONTENTS

INTRODUCTION

"Thank you, God, for the gift of bumbling!" —Bob and Rita

The Focus of This Book

For many years, people—couples, singles, divorced persons and our own children suggested that we should write a book about our marriage. When we finally started the process we asked ourselves what its focus should be. A friend suggested that we should look at what is in the books currently available. We discovered that most of the available literature on marriage is aimed at repairing or saving marriages. While we recognized the value and need for books of this nature, we saw very little for couples in strong marriages who want to enhance and deepen their relationship. Our hope is to assist couples in creating a stronger, more loving relationship. We firmly believe that a strong relationship provides couples with the ability to deal with most of the challenges they face in their lives.

Who We Are

Bob

I grew up in a traditional large Catholic family. I had eleven brothers and sisters. Rita and I met in high school, dated through college and were married in 1966, the summer she graduated from college.

I spent thirty years teaching physics and mathematics in a community college and have done consulting work as well. I retired from college teaching in 1999 and, between 2005 and 2008, taught religion in a Catholic high school.

Rita

I, too, grew up in a traditional Catholic family, slightly smaller than Bob's. We have four grown children—three boys and a girl—and have six grandchildren. While I spent twenty years as a stay at home mom, I have taught religion and history in a Catholic high school for as many years. I have been a campus minister and department chair as well.

Bob and Rita

We have been involved in many Church activities—high school religious education, retreats for teens and liturgy preparation. Bob has worked on teams bringing people into or back to the Church. For many years he wrote a column, *Answering the Call,* on religion in everyday life for various publications. We have presented over a hundred Marriage Encounter weekends and given numerous convention speeches and workshops for married couples, priests and seminarians along with retreats for high school students. We like to read and travel.

We have always been fascinated by the possibilities that marriage provides. Through our more than forty years together, we have explored those possibilities.

Commitment

The story of our lives together is based on the commitment each of us made on our wedding day to love and honor the other in sickness and in health, in good times and bad, so long as we both shall live. For us, there was not to be an end until one of us died. We expected to try everything humanly and divinely possible to live out those promises. Commitment is at the heart of everything we have done in our lives together. It is the reason that we have worked on our relationship and it is in the background of everything we write.

Our Approach to Love

As we begin our story we would like to state a few of the fundamental assumptions that comprise our approach to love and marriage.

While popular songs treat love as a wonderful feeling, love is actually a decision. It is the decision each of us makes to put the well-being of the other ahead of self. This decision may be difficult at times and can be made even when one does not feel very loving. It is possible to love someone even when we dislike them or find them unattractive.

We once saw an actor on television talking about his new girl friend. He was giddy and silly as he described their relationship. After two marriages he claimed that he was finally "in love." From our perception, this forty year old man was infatuated, focused on the good feelings he had about her, seeing her through rose-colored glasses and assuming that the giddiness would last. These are typical behaviors of adolescents and cannot sustain a marriage. We saw no evidence of a realistic understanding of the other person. Nor did we see any sense of the hard work required to build a real relationship that can keep a marriage alive when good feelings fade, as they certainly will at times. Only the decision to love, exercised daily, can sustain a marriage for a lifetime.

While our marriage is kept strong by the daily acts of love we offer to each other, we have always been able to hold on to an element of being "in love," still acting like newlyweds, that adds greatly to the joy in our marriage and makes it easier to live our vows. Nearly everyone we encounter—our children, our students, couples in our workshops find this a little surprising and inviting.

Our Approach to Marriage

We see marriage as having three dimensions. It is first a formal and binding legal contract in which a couple shares financial resources, property and raising children. This is the part of a marriage in which the state has an interest and the reason a marriage license is required. Secondly, it is a covenant. It is established in the solemn promises a couple makes with each other in their wedding vows. They promise before God to be in an exclusive relationship until one of them dies. Thirdly, it is a Sacrament. Living the promises allows God to work in and through them. They and those they affect experience God's love for them.

The legal contract, our forever commitment, and God's grace, help our marriage grow and become the most that it can be only with constant attention. We try to get beyond complacency and look for more. Doing so requires steady effort but it is the source of the most fun and the greatest joy in our lives. This is the story we will tell in this book.

How to Read This Book

We have organized this book so that it can be read both to enjoy our story and to help readers to grow in their own marriages. All of the chapters, except this Introduction and the concluding one, consist of a part of our story followed by a section of Hints, Tips, and Things We've Learned Along the Way. In addition, each chapter has questions to stimulate individual reflection and couple discussion.

There are many ways to use this book. You might just enjoy reading our story. Perhaps you will discover parts of your story in the process. Another approach might be to read each chapter and have a brief dialogue on the questions at the end. For greater benefit we recommend reading a chapter and during the next week use the questions to look deeper into the topic. We have found great benefit in discussing a topic over several days or weeks and have returned to most of the topics and questions multiple times through the years. Each return has brought a new and interesting discussion and greater insights into our lives together.

We recommend that after completing this introductory chapter you read the chapters: "The Beginning of the Dream" and "Staying Connected". The first will help you to reflect on the beginning of your relationship. The second introduces productive ways to communicate in a marriage. The other chapters have only a loose sense of order and may be read in whatever order desired.

As part of growing in our marriage we found it helpful to read a book about marriage together. One of us would read a chapter aloud to the other. We would then discuss what we had heard and consider how we might apply that in our marriage. Those reading this book might try the same. However, if you are reading this and your spouse is not, much of the information we discuss may still be used to the benefit of your marriage.

What This Book Is Not

This is not the story of a perfect marriage. Relationships are inherently "messy" as you will see in our story. Sometimes we thought we knew exactly where we were going and what we wanted our marriage relationship to be, but when we looked back, much of the time we just bumbled along. Fortunately, we found that bumbling means we are in an active relationship and is the real story of our love. For us the bumbling isn't over, we expect it to continue as long as we have breath in us. Thank you, God, for the gift of bumbling!

Everything about our marriage has been influenced by our Catholic Faith and our personal relationships with God. Conversely, each of our relationships with God has been enhanced by our lives together. While we did not include a chapter on faith, prayer or our relationship with God, it will be apparent in our story. We have each grown in our journey with God because of the other, but it is mostly a personal journey for each of us and does not fit the goals of this book. While our faith is important to our story, the stories we tell, the hints and the questions in each chapter can be of benefit to any couple.

We have not included a chapter on children or parenting. Nothing else changed our relationship as much as our children and they enrich our lives more than words can say, but we wanted this book to focus on enhancing marriages, not on parenting.

As you continue the journey with us we invite you to enjoy our story and be inspired to create a marriage that lasts a lifetime. Along the way remember, celebrate and believe in the power of your love.

THE BEGINNING
OF THE DREAM

"Just call me Yogi." —Bob

"I met a girl named Rosie." —Rita

Bob

Marriages are enriched and formed in part by the persons we were when we met and fell in love. This chapter's purpose is to help you to remember the beginning of your journey together.

Many couples like to tell the story of their first meeting. For some it is love at first sight and for others there is an initial dislike or turn-off that they eventually get beyond. We can't start with that story because we don't know when we first met. We both attended the same small high school. Rita was in my sister's class, one year after me. In a small school, everybody knows everybody, especially among the more active students. My first memories of Rita involve activities in things like the Science Club and as my sister's best friend. She was just "around"—and I wasn't interested.

By my senior year I was aware that Rita was interested in me. I remember going on a field trip and she found her way into the same seat on the bus. That was OK—we had a good time—but I wasn't especially interested in dating her, or anybody else, at that time. My focus was on finishing high school and going to college. I expected that I would marry eventually, but I certainly wasn't thinking about a life partner at the time.

During the summer after high school, Rita asked me to go to a family wedding with her and I agreed to our first date. I remember having a good time, but for me she was still mainly my sister's best friend and I didn't ask her for another date.

During my first year of college, I focused on my classes and dated only occasionally. Rita says that I exuded confidence in everything I did, but I was really very shy. I was never good at small talk and the shyness was worse with women. I asked Rita to go to a party with me on New Years Eve, mostly because I didn't know who else to ask.

After New Year's Eve I don't remember seeing Rita again until summer, when she was graduated from high school and I had finished my first year of college. Early that summer we dated a few times. We had good times and that was the beginning of our friendship. I began to see that she was serious and I was getting hooked but I thought I wasn't ready to be dating seriously. We both had college to finish and the prospect of dating for such a long period wasn't attractive to me. I suggested to Rita that we stop seeing each other for a while; we were too young to be so serious. I think she knew that arguing with me wouldn't do much good, so she agreed—with a catch! She asked if we could have just one more date before we went to school in August. I agreed. I think I wanted to continue dating, but didn't want to admit it to myself. After that "one more date", she had me and we never stopped dating. I think it was clear to me rather quickly that we would get married. I remember a time, not too long after, when we were riding in the car and talking about something and I said, " When we are married…" but quickly changed it to "If we get married…". I wasn't quite ready to admit it, but there wasn't any doubt.

Fortunately, Rita knew what she wanted and wouldn't let go. I might have walked away from the best person to ever come into my life.

During our college years I was in Dayton and Rita in Cincinnati. We saw each other when we could both get home for a weekend or I could get a ride to Cincinnati with a friend. When we were apart we wrote each other a letter nearly every day. We liked to talk on the telephone, but couldn't afford the pay phone in the dorm very often.

When we were together we were playful and frequently kidded each other. One evening we were goofing around and Rita made a remark about me being either very smart or a smart-aleck. I can't remember which. My response was to say: "Just call me Yogi." When she looked puzzled I added: "Smarter than the average bear," in reference to the cartoon character. "Yogi" became her pet name for me, especially when I was being goofy.

It was great to get the occasional phone call, but letters became the staple of our communication. During the year before we were married, I was in graduate school in Illinois and we didn't get to see each other very often. I wasn't satisfied with just letters. I was always inclined to solve problems with technology (the word "geek" hadn't been invented yet), so I bought two small, reel-to-reel tape recorders (cassettes hadn't been invented, either) and several tapes. We would tape our letters so that we could listen to each other's voices. I looked forward to Rita's letters—I wanted to know everything that was happening in her life—but hearing her voice on tape was special.

At the beginning, I saw the long dating period we were facing as an obstacle, but I look back on it now as the time during which our friendship developed. We didn't have either money or opportunity to spend a lot of time focused on anything outside of us. We had many, many hours to discuss our hopes and dreams for us, careers, children and the home we would like to have some day.

When I went back to school for my sophomore year I was committed to Rita. She was the person I intended to marry and I no longer had any interest in anyone else. In January of that year, I gave her my high school ring and asked her to marry me. I have vivid memories of my ring on her finger wrapped in fuzzy pale blue yarn to make it fit.

I was slow to develop an interest in Rita, but as time went on it was obvious that we enjoyed each other's company. I have always been a smart-aleck and Rita appreciated my sense of humor. She is smart and sensitive and very good with people. She also shared my dreams. I knew when I was rather young that I wasn't cut out to be a farmer, as my father was. I wanted to get an education and a job that would challenge me intellectually. Having children was important to me. My family had a tradition of involvement in the Church and I wanted to continue that tradition. Rita was with me in all these things and we had many discussions about them during our college years.

From the first time I kissed Rita there was a sexual tension and a strong desire. Not only was I a healthy teenage male, I found this female very desirable. We discussed sexual issues, along with many other things. One decision we made was that we would not have sex until we were married. It's not that no-body was doing it—we knew couples who were hurrying up their wedding to be married before the baby arrived. I believed, as I still do, that it is morally wrong and I wanted to do nothing that would interfere with completing my education. Fortunately, Rita agreed with me and was even more determined than I to wait.

Along the way there always seemed to be people to support us and help us to go in the right direction. My mother encouraged us to pray together and we took her suggestion. It was one of the things that reminded us to continue to do what was right with and toward each other.

The telephone on my dorm floor was just outside Father Matt's room. When Rita called me he would often answer the phone and question her about who she was and give her a hard time about why he should call me to the phone. While he was kidding, the undertone was always clearly one of caring. He knew us and wanted us to succeed. We don't know why he remembered this story, but until he died he told this to new students at the university when he found out that they knew one of us. Father Matt also suggested that we have our engagement blessed, and we did.

During Rita's senior year of college we prepared for our wedding in August. This happened while she was in Cincinnati and I was in Chicago. In October, high school friends of ours were married in Ohio. We were not yet formally engaged so I went shopping for a ring. I was living on a very limited budget but with the help of a friend I found a jeweler and a ring I could afford. On my way to Ohio that weekend I stopped at a florist and purchased a dozen roses, eleven red and one white. I presented Rita the roses with her engagement ring in the white rose. (I'm an incurably romantic geek!)

Rita took care of most of the details of planning our wedding. She kept me informed in the letters she wrote. I finished my Masters Degree the week before our wedding and then we finished all the last minute details together. I didn't have a lot to do the morning of our wedding. I delivered my car to the best man's house since we were going to change there to leave for our honeymoon. I was eager for the ceremony to begin. I remember waiting at the altar as Rita's brother escorted her down the aisle. She was breathtakingly beautiful in her long white wedding gown. I still think so when I look at our wedding pictures. When we exchanged our vows I was eager to make the commitment. I tried to say "I will" loudly enough that everyone in church would hear me.

The reception went fairly quickly for me. We were kept busy greeting family and friends. All the time I was waiting for the moment when we could say goodbye to our parents and get away from the crowd. The thing I wanted most was to be alone with Rita.

It was a special moment at the best man's house, when I helped Rita out of her wedding gown and we changed clothes together for the first time in our lives. Rita sat close to me in the car as we drove the twenty miles to a small motel. We continued to take my mother's advice and knelt beside the bed to pray.

Our honeymoon was a wonderful celebration of being together and enjoying the friendship we had developed during our dating years. The added dimension of an active sexual relationship made it extra special and allowed us to start our marriage with growth toward new depth. Waiting was worth it.

We honeymooned in a cabin in Kentucky that gave us all the privacy newlyweds wanted. We didn't even have to worry about the maids wanting to make up our room. Each morning when we woke up we found new towels and linens on the porch of our cabin but no one ever knocked on the door.

I was crazy in love with Rita. She gave me her entire attention. It was fun to take a paddle boat ride around the lake and walk in the woods. It didn't matter what we were doing, I just loved to be with her.

We had often talked about what our marriage would be like and were determined that it would be one of the best marriages of all time. On our honeymoon we made three promises to each other. The first was to say "I love you!" every day of our lives. The second was never to leave each other for more than a few minutes without kissing each other goodbye. Our third promise was that we would always go to sleep at night with some part of our bodies touching. It was to be a reminder that we are lovers, no matter what else is going on in our lives. After more than forty years of marriage we continue to live these promises.

During the early years of our marriage I was in graduate school and Rita was teaching. We were a six hour drive from our nearest family member. We made friends with Rita's co-workers but we still had lots of time just for us. Not knowing many people forced us to rely on each other for companionship and helped our friendship to grow even more.

There was a very heavy snowstorm in Chicago during January of our first year. I had come home from classes and found the roads nearly impassable. Rita was still at school, so I went there, walked into the principal's office, and announced that I was taking Rita home, whether she liked it or not. I wasn't about to have Rita stranded in the snow away from our apartment. We just managed to get back home before all the streets were closed and thus were able to enjoy being snowed in for several days.

In those first years of our marriage I worked on a doctorate and found myself moving toward the goals I had dreamed about. Since I was taking courses and spending lots of time studying, I was busy, but my schedule was flexible. It allowed us more time together than another job would have. On Friday afternoons I often met Rita after school and we would go out for beer and burgers with the other young teachers from her high school. I enjoyed the freedom we had to come and go during those years.

Rita

We each have our own memories of how our relationship began. So here is my story. During my freshman year of high school I met a girl named Rosie. We quickly developed a friendship that has lasted to today. As our friendship grew, I learned that she had an older brother. While I don't remember officially meeting Bob, I became interested in him. Rosie didn't seem to mind. Most teens in our school were not allowed to date one on one until we were sixteen so we hung around in various groups that attended school or community activities. During that time I became attracted to things about Bob. He was definitely cute, extremely intelligent, ranking at the top of his class, was always neatly dressed, and looking back, he seemed very self assured. He had dreams for his life and was determined to get there. I liked what he wanted for his life and realized that it was what I wanted, too. As we did all the normal things teens did then, I found myself more and more interested in him. He didn't seem interested in me so Rosie and I began to plot various ways to pique his interest. On occasion he would show interest. One night he drove me home from a school dance and another time he slipped a few pieces of candy on my desk. Even though he seemed to most often see me as Rosie's friend, I was aware of an attraction between us and I found myself falling in love with him. During the summer after my junior year, I asked him for our first date. We had a great time and we saw each other a few times but he was caught up in college preparation. I began my senior year of high school and even dated a few other boys. I thought about him and Rosie kept me posted on what he was doing. He asked me to celebrate New Year's Eve with him. I didn't see him again until the night I graduated when he took a picture of me as I gave my graduation speech. Not long after, a copy of that picture arrived in the mail with a note saying he would call me soon. We had a few dates that June and there was a definite chemistry developing between us. We shared common interests and could talk for hours or just be together and say nothing. A casual relationship suddenly seemed to be serious. Near the end of June Bob decided that we were getting too serious too fast and that with college ahead for both of us, we should not see each other. I suggested that we have one more date in late August before we both went to college. He agreed. We saw each other casually the next few weeks and then he asked me for a date. I don't remember what we did but I do remember that we were standing on the front porch of my mother's house and he kissed me goodnight several times and then quickly said "I love you" and ran to his car. That was the beginning of the rest of our life together. Whether we were too serious or not, both of us knew that we were interested in a future together even if we didn't say it. We dated every weekend the rest of that summer and started to dream together about where we wanted life to take us.

We both went off to college in separate cities, promising to write frequently and see each other when we could go home for weekends. It was with great anticipation that I checked my mailbox each day. Being a starry eyed teenager, I was always looking for signs that would tell me that Bob was the right person for me. One of those signs came to me through my college roommate. Of all the people that could have been my roommate, I discovered through conversations that the pastor of her parish was Bob's uncle.

As we left for college we didn't make any promises to each other about being exclusively faithful, although it was likely in the back of each of our minds. I went to a few college mixers that first semester. I found myself comparing every boy I met to Bob and no one measured up to him. Eventually I just stopped going.

College life was very busy for me. I took a lot of credit hours that first semester and had work study and another job. Bob was never far from my thoughts but he wasn't the only focus in my life. I always wanted to be a teacher and I was determined to make that happen. Distance was a mixed blessing. It was difficult to be apart and yet it gave each of us the freedom to accomplish things that we both wanted in our lives. Whenever we managed to get together, there were not enough hours in the day or night to talk. Bob's dad was concerned about what the neighbors would say when he got home at 2 or 3 in the morning and one of his little brothers wanted to know why he didn't just sleep at my house since he spent more time there than he did at home.

During those four years, our love for each other grew. I was then and am still now amazed and frequently surprised by the little things he does that show his love for me. It started with the candy in high school, then the wild roses he picked along the roadside, to the roses with my engagement ring, to the Pepsi and Tootsie Rolls in the wee hours of the morning on our wedding night. He made and makes me feel loved and cherished.

Being on scholarships and working to pay college expenses never left us with much money to spend on dates. At home we frequently attended wedding receptions of family and friends or drive-in movies and public dances. On dates at school we roamed through bookstores and furniture sections in department stores. Frequently, we would end up at the Cathedral in Cincinnati for Mass or to receive the Sacrament of Reconciliation. While much of this may not seem exciting by today's standards, it was definitely part of the dreaming that is part of our relationship.

I looked forward to Bob having his arm around me at the movie, or hugging and kissing as we sat in the car, or merely holding hands as we walked through stores. My students roll their eyes when we are studying dating and marriage and I bring up the subject of sex outside of marriage. Somehow they believe that it was so much easier to not have sex when we were dating. I tell them that we had exactly the same decision to make as they do. We had many opportunities and places to have sex had we wanted to do so. I was definitely determined in this area. Growing up I was taught that it was wrong and I wanted nothing to get in the way of my college education. Another motivation I had was I did not want to embarrass my mother. She worked very hard as a young widow to support us and I respected her and didn't want to add to the difficulties she faced as a single parent. The decision was not easily made or only made once. We even talked about it the Sunday night before we were married. Having waited that long we decided another week could be tolerated. Waiting made for an incredible wedding night and honeymoon.

During the four years we dated, I did all the dreamy things that a young lover does. When I look back at college notebooks I find hearts with Bob and Rita or Bob loves Rita or Bob and

Rita Boeke written in the margins. I remember how my heart would skip a beat when someone knocked on my dorm door or yelled down the dorm hallway that I had a phone call. We began to make wedding plans the summer after Bob graduated from college and I began the count down when it was 365 days. Every letter that I wrote him had the number somewhere on it. We became engaged in October. I only had to tell a few people when I went back to school before it spread throughout the dorm. Even a few of the religious sisters had heard and stopped to see my engagement ring and ask about our marriage plans.

We never considered not having a Church wedding. I spent the summer preparing for it. Before I knew it I was being escorted down the aisle by my brother. I remember thinking how young and innocent Bob looked as I walked down the aisle. Bob's uncles witnessed our vows and we were off to a whirlwind reception. The day passed quickly as we celebrated with friends and family, posed for pictures and were congratulated by everyone important in our lives.

In some of our chats before we were married we had talked about what we thought our wedding night would be. I'm not sure any amount of discussion could have prepared me for the intimacy that began to develop that night. We talked and celebrated our commitment to each other. Bob's ability to do little things for me even came through that night. Having been the nervous, busy bride I hadn't eaten much all day. Somewhere in the wee hours of the morning I was starving and he got dressed and tried to find something for me to eat. He came back with a bottle of Pepsi and some Tootsie Rolls. Both will forever have a special place in my heart.

Our honeymoon was wonderful. We swam, laid in the sun, played scrabble and made love to each other. Each day I fell more and more in love with him. Never before in my life could I remember having been that much the center of some-one else's life. When we arrived in Chicago to live I knew no one but Bob. I was suddenly responsible for taking care of an apartment, planning meals, etc. In a few weeks I started my career as a teacher in a school that I had only visited for an interview. Bob settled in as a doctoral student. We didn't have a lot of material possessions but liked our little apartment and life together. Those early years were carefree as Bob went to classes and I truly enjoyed being a teacher. We lived away from our families and old friends so our friendship continued to grow and we made new friends.

Having children was always something that we knew we wanted to do. We picked out a boy's and girl's name when we dated. As the years passed we had four. Being married to my special "Yogi" was wonderful.

Hints, Tips and Things We Learned Along the Way

The tips at the end of each chapter are the starting point for you to begin the process of enriching your relationship.

The following suggestions are offered to assist you as you remember who you were and why you wanted to spend your lives together. Try some of these activities.

* Plan a romantic evening together. Start with a candlelight dinner using your china and crystal or order a pizza and have a beer together. Take out your wedding album and/or video and spend some time remembering who you were then and how you felt about each other.

* Spend an evening going through pictures of your dating years.

* Park outside your first house or apartment and reminisce about the good things that happened while you lived there. While you are there, drive around the neighborhood and look up some other memories.

* Tell your children how you met and share some stories about some of the crazy/fun things you did when you were dating.

* Renew your vows to each other, either alone or publicly.

Questions to Help Guide Your Discussion/ Dialogue

Remember to share the feelings that go with the memories.

1. Where did I find me/us in Bob and Rita's story?

2. What did I like most about you when we dated? Why was I attracted to you?

3. When and where did I know that I wanted to spend the rest of my life with you? Be as specific as you can.

4. What dreams do I remember having for our future together as we prepared for marriage? What has happened to those dreams?

5. What did I learn about you on our honeymoon?

6. What is the most intimate and/or fun moment I remember from our honeymoon?

7. What promises, if any, did we make to each other as we were preparing for our wedding or on our honeymoon? How are we living or not living those promises?

8. Why would I want to marry you again today?

STAYING CONNECTED

...why I don't want to wear it." —Rita

"grunts, sighs, giggles and sobs" —Bob

The Technique

Rita

When couples get married, they have dreams of living happily ever after and believe they will stay together forever. From what we have lived, observed, and read, this is difficult to do without help. Staying connected the way we envisioned on our wedding day requires various kinds of support. For us it has come from our families who value marriage, from friends who share that same vision, from our religious convictions and from opportunities that have presented themselves through the years. Some of these opportunities have been books we read, workshops and retreats we've attended and conversations with friends and loved ones. An important opportunity for us came in the form of a weekend retreat for married couples called Marriage Encounter. One conclusion we can draw from all that we have experienced is the necessity for good verbal communication. It is the key to staying connected. It makes me vulnerable and challenges me to grow as an individual as well as in my relationship with Bob. It gives me opportunities to get to know myself and allows Bob to get to know me in ways I didn't imagine on our wedding day. The result is a closeness and intimacy that we dreamed of then and now work to experience every day.

On that Marriage Encounter weekend we were taught a communication technique that we have used throughout most of our marriage. We select a topic, reflect individually, share our thoughts and feelings and discuss together. While this technique has worked for us and many other couples, it is not the only method for successful marital communication. Try this method or find a method that works for you.

In our culture we often use the word feeling to convey two meanings, an emotional response or an opinion. In our communication we use the word feeling to indicate an emotional response. Not recognizing the distinction between opinions and feelings may create problems in communication. A trick we learned to help us recognize the difference is the following. If I say "I feel" followed by the word "that", it is an opinion. For instance, I feel that most people who drive SUV's are aggressive. This opinion may be the result of something I have read on the subject or my personal experience as a driver. I can just as easily say "I think that" or "I believe that" and it still conveys the same information. When stating my emotional response I say "I feel" followed by a feeling word. Feeling words convey emotion. I feel happy, sad, angry, joyful, lonely, ecstatic, helpless or peaceful to name

a few. I can substitute "am" and the meaning is the same.
I am happy or I am lonely. To illustrate, I **think** SUV driv-
ers are aggressive and I **am** uncomfortable following them as
I drive.

Having feelings is one of the things that make us human.
Sometimes I am more aware of them than others and some
feelings are stronger than others. On occasion I may not like
the feelings I have or wish I felt the way someone else does.
Even when I don't think I have a feeling, I do. I just may have
difficulty naming it.

While we can change our opinions and our thoughts on
a subject, our feelings just occur. My feelings may change
with further communication, information, knowledge, or
life experience but I can't make them change. The reason for
sharing my feelings is not to change them but to let Bob know
that unique part of me. Since feelings just happen, there are
not appropriate or inappropriate ones to have. I may wish
I had other feelings at times, but try as I may, I can't make
myself have certain feelings in a given situation. Bob may
give me a gift of an article of clothing. I may be very grateful and appreciative of the gift and the sentiment behind it,
feel happy about receiving it, but I can't make myself be excited if it somehow doesn't strike me as something I'd like to
wear. My response to receiving the gift can, however, have
an appropriate or inappropriate action. I could make some
negative comment in his presence, which would definitely be
inappropriate, or thank him and explain why I don't want to
wear it. I might even suggest that we go shopping together.
If I am upset about something and feel angry or discouraged,
Bob may hug me and ask if he can do anything to help me.
I can respond with angry words and push him away or say
thanks, but not now. Once again, it's good to remember that

feelings are neither right nor wrong, they just are. However, actions in a response to a feeling may be right or wrong. Identifying my feelings and accepting them as part of who I am has helped me to decide what course of action to take in most situations. A final comment: obviously I want to have positive feelings more than negative ones. Frequent negative feelings about certain issues in our life may indicate the need for more reflection and discussion in that area.

Bob

The communication technique which Rita introduced was part of our daily lives for more than 25 years. It consists of three parts: question/topic, reflection/writing and dialogue/discussion. There are many techniques, but this worked well for us.

Growth in a marriage is strongly enhanced through repeated communication on a variety of subjects. This technique assumes that there is a desire to discuss a particular topic or issue. The first step is to agree on the topic or issue for reflection and dialogue. We phrase the subject in the form of a question. We might use a question like: "What are my thoughts and feelings now about our disagreement the other night?" or "What are my thoughts and feelings about my favorite memory from our vacation?" We provide many such questions at the end of each of the chapters of this book.

We each write a letter to the other person describing our thoughts and feelings about the subject. This reflection time is ten minutes or so, longer if needed. We write it in letter form starting with a loving greeting and refer to our writing as love letters. This helps us to remember that we are lovers and enables us to disagree with each other or say something that is difficult without being critical or blaming. It is helpful to describe feelings, as discussed in Rita's section.   When I name and describe a feeling for Rita, I avoid blaming her for my emotional response.   It is my feeling and I take responsibility for it.   As a result I can say, "I feel annoyed <u>when</u> you leave the wet dish sponge in the sink," but I would not say: "I feel annoyed <u>because</u> you left the wet sponge in the sink."   The value of this written reflection is that it allows me to think about what I want to say and take the time to say it carefully so that she will hear me and not be hurt by it.   It keeps me from seeing an expression on her face that might cause me to change my mind.   In writing I have made a commitment to share this with Rita and our communication has the potential to deepen.

The dialogue can take place in a variety of situations, but we prefer to make time and find a quiet, private place where we will not be interrupted.   This can be difficult with small children but it is worth trying and perhaps achieving some of the time.   We exchange our letters and I read Rita's letter twice to get the full flavor of the feelings and thoughts she has shared with me.   After reading, we have a discussion about the contents of our letters.   Sometimes we wander off on another topic quickly and at other times we discuss for hours.

When we recognized that we could share our thoughts and feelings in our daily conversation we stopped using the formal technique.   We return to it when we come upon a subject that is especially difficult to discuss.

Most methods of communication include active listening.   It involves paying careful attention to the words of another and then feeding back what you have heard to see if it matches what was meant.   It includes asking questions to clarify anything that is not clear.   Each time, the speaker responds to the feedback with any needed clarification.

Non-Verbal Communication

Any time we are in the presence of another person there is communication. Sometimes we use words – verbal communication - and sometimes we get information from the body language – posture or facial expression, sounds – grunts, sighs, giggles and sobs that make up non-verbal communication. We may not be conscious of non-verbal communication, but we respond to it anyway. Many times I decide to change what I say to Rita when I see anger or disappointment start to appear on her face. If I am talking to Rita about something that is important to me and she slouches in her chair or drums her fingers on the table, I find it hard to believe that she is listening to me. When Rita calls me she sometimes can tell that I am distracted and not actually listening when I am slow to respond to the things she is saying. It is even worse when she can hear the clicking of my computer keys.

Non-verbal communication is always present. It can't be turned off. It is more useful in our communication when we are aware of it and when we actively work with it. It can be difficult to know the meaning of a facial expression or other sign. When Rita has a certain little grin on her face as she is about to speak, I know that I will likely enjoy what will follow, but I have no idea what it is. If I am in the process of telling her something and see her frown, I suspect that she doesn't like something I'm saying, but I can't be sure. Maybe she just remembered that she didn't pick up the dry cleaning. In these situations we have both learned to check it out. I might say: "Why the frown? Is it something I said?"

When there is a mismatch between the words we hear and the non-verbal cues we see, we tend to give more credibility to the non-verbal. As the last example shows, body language isn't always more reliable, so it is important to conduct a verbal check. Paying conscious attention to both verbal and non-verbal communication and running verbal checks on what I hear and observe are a part of active listening and are important to clear communication.

Hints, Tips and Things We Learned Along the Way

Ideas to enhance your communication:

- ❖ Choose or create the proper environment for both the reflection and discussion. Some couples find it important to always reflect and discuss in the same place. We wrote most anywhere and usually discussed in our bedroom. We found ways to use the technique when we were camping with the kids, under a street lamp before going into a party and by candlelight in front of the fireplace. Most importantly, we recommend that it be done when and where you are least likely to be interrupted.

- ❖ The discussion time needs to be mutually agreed upon. It is not fair to expect your spouse to listen, much less engage in significant discussion, while s/he is watching their favorite television program or sporting event. We mutually decide the time.

- ❖ Communication of any kind may cause tension. This is especially true if you're being interrupted while you are speaking, if you can't understand the other's feelings or don't agree with your partner's thoughts and opinions. It might also create stress and tension when you realize there is something about yourself that you need to change or when you want to fix your spouse. It is important to remember that the purpose of communication is to get to know the other person, not fix them.

❋   This method may not be right for every couple. There are numerous communication techniques available. Find one that works for the two of you or make adaptations to our method. Just keep talking.

❋   Remember the process is a tool, not an end in itself. If one or both of you keeps focusing on doing it right, you will be frustrated and likely not continue with the technique. Don't forget that the objective is to achieve greater intimacy by getting to know the other person more fully.

❋   Since the objective is greater intimacy, it needs to be used frequently. We used it daily and it helped us stay close through the ups and downs of our lives. Having shared our feelings in the communication process, we could then continue the discussion and resolve differences, avoid conflict and celebrate joyful moments. Some couples used it only when they needed to problem solve. We think they missed some of the joyful moments that we have been able to share. Frequently, they lost the commitment to using the technique

❋   During the individual reflection time we used
    a few moments for prayer, usually in writing,
    and as part of the discussion time we began
    with a few moments of prayer.

❋   It is important to recognize that every mar-
    ried couple needs a support structure. You
    need to have some people in your life who
    support marriage and your marriage in par-
    ticular. Look for people who can support and
    encourage you on your journey.

❋   Intimacy requires trust and honesty. Don't
    share everything through rose colored glasses
    nor with brutal descriptions. Choose words
    carefully and respect what your spouse is try-
    ing to convey. The feelings that accompany
    the thoughts, opinions, assumptions, etc.,
    are there - it merely takes practice to convey
    them so that your relationship can grow and
    not be destroyed.

❋   Many today rely on electronic communication.
    It is a wonderful way to transfer information.
    However, to build a deep intimacy, not merely
    the transfer of information, requires a physi-
    cal presence and attention for most of your
    discussions.

❋   If you would like more information about the
    weekend we attended or where you might
    attend one in your area, contact Worldwide

Marriage Encounter at www.wwme.org or call 909.863.9963.

❋ If, after working to strengthen your communication, you still feel distant from each other rather than close or have not been able to resolve any differences, perhaps it is time to seek professional help. We would recommend that you do so either individually or as a couple.

Ideas that might help you to be an active listener:

❋ Don't say anything until your spouse is finished. Don't interrupt no matter how strongly you might want to reply, whether you agree or disagree.

❋ When your partner is finished, you may need to ask questions to help clarify and get more information. Then do the same for the other.

❋ When you think you understand what has been communicated, try to feed back what you heard.

❋ If your partner says that your feedback is not what was intended then he/she needs to state it again with more or different detail.

❋ Recognize through the entire process that your body language might have an effect on the trust and confidence needed by your spouse to convey what s/he is trying to say.

Questions to Help Guide Your Discussion/ Dialogue

Remember to share your feelings as you respond to each question.

1. What are my thoughts and feelings about the way we communicate?

2. Did I find anything in Bob and Rita's "Staying Connected" that I think would be helpful to us?

3. Am I aware of my feelings and do I communicate them?

4. Describe a time when my feelings had either a positive or negative affect on our relationship.

5. What makes it easy for me to share my feelings and what makes it difficult?

6. Do I find it easy to share some feeling and not others?

7. Am I willing to make a commitment to work on communication in our marriage?

8. Did I find anything in Bob and Rita's "Staying Connected" that I would like to try?

9. Who or what supports our marriage the most?
   How do I experience that support? Do we need
   to find more people or opportunities that will
   support our marriage?

WHEN DREAMS COME TRUE

"...harder than I imagined it would be." — Bob

"...wonderful and yet it wasn't." — Rita

Bob

During our dating years and early marriage we discussed nearly everything. We talked about the future of my education, the children we hoped for, our dream house, what our sex life would be like and the jobs we would have. I think we even talked about where we wanted to live when we retire. It is easy for me to do that. I always have several things I would like to do and look forward to getting started. I'm a dreamer.

When we were married, I dreamed about the day I would be the first member of my family to receive a doctoral degree and how my parents would be proud of me. I spent the first two years of our marriage as a doctoral student. I had some problems with my dissertation committee and the research didn't go as well as I had hoped, but I expected to get the degree - just a little later than planned. With time, events in our lives pressed me to get a job and made it harder to complete the work. Eventually I decided, with Rita's help, to stop pursuing the degree in favor of other dreams.

Children were always a part of my dreams. With my large family, I couldn't imagine going through life without children. I thought I wanted to be like my parents and have a dozen. After a few years of marriage and no children we began to worry about fertility issues and talked to doctors about possibilities. Along the way we discussed adoption. I strongly hoped to have biological children, but was open to adoption if that was our only alternative. With some medical assistance we eventually found ourselves expecting a child and eagerly awaiting his birth. I was fascinated by the changes in Rita's body and thrilled when she put my hand on her expanding middle and I could feel the baby move.

He was a great joy. I was fascinated by how small and fragile he seemed and naively surprised by the time and energy it took to care for him. As he grew and learned to respond to me I couldn't get enough of playing with him. I loved helping him to learn to crawl and walk and was quite proud of myself when I taught him to go safely down stairs.

My dream job was to teach in a university and do research in education, which required that I finish my degree. Before I could do that our family financial situation made it necessary for me to get a job. I was invited to apply for a community college teaching job in my undergraduate fields of physics and mathematics. I found myself enjoying the teaching and an experienced teacher who observed me in the classroom told me that I was very good. A group of seasoned faculty encouraged me to become involved in the Faculty Senate, which meant campus politics. I was soon involved in high-profile committees and receiving lots of affirmation from my colleagues. The educational research I wanted to do became very hands-on as I experimented with teaching methods in my own classroom.

While we were expecting our second child we decided that we needed more space and began to look for a house. I knew that it wasn't our dream house, but it was a step in that direction. It was a rather small house, but I remember being in awe that we could live in such a nice place. After a couple of years I finished the lower level and made it even nicer.

Our dreams were coming true, substantially as we had envisioned them. We had children, a nice house and I had a great job. Rita was able to stay home with the kids. Everything should have been wonderful. But it wasn't perfect.

I had my dissertation hanging over me and wasn't making much progress. I still gave it some of my time but even when I didn't work on it for a while it was always there and was a drain on my energy. While I still have occasional regrets about dropping the degree, it wasn't necessary for me to have a great life.

My job was demanding. I was always trying new things in my classes that took time and energy to prepare. The committees I served on and sometimes chaired involved considerable time beyond meetings. Most evenings I worked after dinner on class preparation or paper grading and frequently took calls related to my committee work.

Rita was up at night with the kids, especially when they were very small and she was nursing them. That, combined with our natural tendency to be on different time schedules, meant that she was frequently in bed and asleep before me.

Our intimate communication began to slip. Eventually I realized that we didn't seem to be having as much fun as before.

I missed our talks but it seemed that when I was ready she was tired or asleep or one of the kids needed something. When she was ready I was busy, mostly with my job. We still talked, but more about the house, kids and finances than about us. When we did talk, I tended to interpret her tired-ness and distraction as a lack of interest. At these times I was lonely, but didn't know what to do about it. I still loved her but I thought that she might no longer find me interesting or desirable. I didn't blame her but wondered what was wrong with me. I was afraid to push it because I didn't want to risk confirmation that my fears were true.

It wasn't that we were never close. Sometimes we found time to be intimate and dream together. Then I felt close to Rita and my loneliness faded away. Life overall was still good. It was great that our dreams were happening, but keeping the joy and fun alive in us was harder than I imagined it would be. It was ironic that our wonderful dreams created some of our greatest obstacles.

Rita

Being married was wonderful, we never had to say good-night and separate. Now we just said goodnight as we lay next to each other. We'd wake up and start each new day together. It was great to just enjoy the silence when we were each reading, or the discussions we had as we tried to figure out the best place to put our wedding gifts, or how to deco-rate our apartment on our limited budget. We laughed at ourselves as we adjusted to living with another person, cried on occasion when we discussed infertility and Bob's frustra-tion over not being able to finish his dissertation. We had fun when we bought our first "new" car and convinced our-selves that a convertible probably was not practical. We were fascinated by the changes in my body when I became pregnant and shared ideas about parenting. We talked about where we would live when Bob finished school and when we would be able to get a house of our own. I knew we were right for each other and our unfolding dreams seemed to support that. I was not prepared for the unexpected changes that happened when those dreams became a reality or didn't work out exactly as I thought.

A great job fell into Bob's life. He enjoyed it and quickly gained respect from his colleagues. He was very busy preparing lessons, grading papers and getting involved in committee work and faculty issues. At the same time he was trying to finish writing his dissertation. When I met his colleagues, I felt very proud when they would tell me about all the wonderful things he was doing.

Those children we had talked about and named when we were dating came as well. With a little help from medical science, I became pregnant. Pregnancy was easy for me and we had fun with the changes in my body and doing all the things we needed to do to prepare for the baby's birth. We were very relaxed with it all. I quit teaching when our first child was born. At times I missed teaching and being with the young adults on the faculty, but many of them had moved on to other things in their lives as well. My life was filled with doing all the things I thought motherhood entailed. I couldn't wait to call Bob or tell him when he got home about all the things the baby had learned to do. I loved being a mother even if I didn't always know what I was doing. Two years later I became pregnant again.

About this time we even managed to get a house of our own. On a whim, we put $10 down on a house with two weeks to think about it. Every spare minute of those two weeks was spent looking at the floor plans and figuring out how we could live in that house. Bob worked the numbers over and over again to see if we could finance it. We bought the house and went to watch its construction nearly every night. We couldn't wait to move in.

As our dreams became realities our world expanded. I loved being a mother but having children required great expenditures of time and energy. Having a new house was wonderful. Wedding gifts we had never used came out of boxes, arranging and rearranging furniture was fun. But it now required more time to keep it clean than our small apartment had. We moved into a new neighborhood in which I knew no one. I missed the companionship of the other women in the apartment building. We had stretched our budget to get the house and the addition of another child stretched it even more. The new couples we met were very different than we had been used to. Everything was wonderful and yet it wasn't. With the expansion in our responsibilities, we had not figured out how to adjust our communication to fit the changes. We talked - but more about practical things than dreaming. We enjoyed each other but there wasn't time to do little things for and with each other and I missed being the center of Bob's time and attention.

Part of me wasn't surprised by this. Most of our married friends seemed to be going through the same thing. It was that settling down time that everyone talked about. We communicated major things to each other but little things sometimes got lost along the way. As Bob's job expanded he seemed happy. I tried to adjust to the loneliness I felt when he was busy. I filled my days with reading when I got a chance to read, and spent more time with the sewing machine and our children than I did with him. Seeing all the things I sewed or the things the kids learned and the fun I had in the process covered the loneliness much of the time. I knew Bob was often frustrated with the lack of physical intimacy that we had once shared, as was I, but there just wasn't enough time to fit everything into our day. Special time together seemed to be the easiest thing to let slide. I knew I loved Bob and that he loved me but it just wasn't quite the same. I looked around at what we had, all the dreams seemed to have come true, and yet, I couldn't figure out what was missing. Sometimes I was envious of Bob's ability to get out of the house while I was mired in diapers and dust bunnies; after all I had a college degree as well. We only had one car and it took much arrangement in schedules for me to use it. Yet at other times when we could share dreams, joys and frustrations with each other, it was like dating and our early marriage and everything was okay.

Fortunately for us, the Marriage Encounter weekend helped us to refocus our lives. We had time for just each other without jobs, children or houses to think about. We revisited dreams and began to create some new plans for a future together while we expressed some of our frustrations with the reality of our lives. Revisiting the reality of dreams through the years has helped us live with much of the closeness we envisioned when we were married.

Hints, Tips and Things We Learned Along the Way

* All relationships have ups and downs. Loneliness or loss of closeness may begin to appear after 5-7 years of marriage, especially as the dreams you had when you were married are becoming the daily reality. We have heard it referred to as disillusionment, spiritual divorce or the seven year itch.

* Your dreams are ideals and viewed through rose colored glasses. The reality requires each of you to see through clearer glasses.

* Loneliness or loss of closeness will happen multiple times in your relationship. Having these feelings does not mean that your marriage is over. Recognizing the loss of closeness is the first step in working through it and presents you with an opportunity to revive the dreams you had or create new ones.

* There is more than one way to deal with the lack of closeness in your relationship but developing better communication skills is essential.

* When things are going well we take for granted our closeness and forget to maintain it.

* Some times the feelings of loneliness come slowly and other times they come charging at us. Usually we are surprised.

* The person you married is more important than any dream. Some dreams may need to be let go.

* Don't stop dreaming. One of the things that keeps a relationship alive is the ability to dream together. Choose a specific time, perhaps each year on your anniversary, to revisit dreams.

Questions to Help Guide Your Discussion/ Dialogue

Remember to share your feelings as you respond to the questions.

1. Where did I find me/us in Bob and Rita's story?

2. Do I ever experience feelings of loneliness in our relationship? Describe them.

3. What keeps me from feeling close to you? Why do I think it does that?

4. What dreams did I have for us when we were married?

5. Which of my dreams have come true? Has the effect been what I expected?

6. What dreams have I abandoned? Why?

7. When was the last time we shared dreams with each other?

8. What dreams do I have for us today?

LITTLE THINGS MEAN A LOT

"…gets the color and options she wants…" — Bob

"…a peach gives me the creeps." — Rita

Bob

The end of a marriage often results from many small annoyances that are repeated over and over and some that are simply ignored. In the same way, a marriage is greatly enhanced by small, loving acts of kindness and caring that are unexpected and never demanded. When both are committed to the relationship, keeping the spark alive comes from the caring and respect shown in small, unexpected actions that make us feel loved and appreciated.

Rita is not very interested in cars and how they operate. When we buy a car that she will drive, I do the background work before we shop. When we bought a car for Rita, I saw one that appeared suitable. I told the salesman that I was looking for a car for my wife. She met me at the dealer, sat in it, checked the options and color and went home. Our son and I took the car for a test drive. As I was negotiating the deal, the salesman suddenly stopped and said, "I thought this car was for your wife?!" I assured him that it was. Normally, I test drive the car, make the decision and negotiate the deal. She gets the color and options she wants without any worry about the suitability of the car and negotiating a good deal. The extra bonus is that while it is her car, I drive the car fairly often so in effect I have two cars I like.

A few years ago, we became aware of a problem with the regularity of my heartbeat. The doctors checked me out and concluded that it is not life-threatening and something I can live with without any serious effect on my lifestyle. I learned to live my life without great concern and worry. The same is not true for Rita, but I didn't know the extent of her fears until the day I fell asleep on the bed while doing some exercises. After a time she realized that I was very quiet and came to the room to check on me. She told me how she checked first to be sure that I was breathing and then woke me up. As we were discussing this incident, she shared with me how concerned she gets when she thinks that I am at home and I don't answer the phone or she can't get through to my cell phone. While I'm sorry for the stress this causes her, her concern makes me feel very much loved and I am honored by her caring.

Both of us have a rule of never talking negatively about the other to anyone. When we are in groups and the conversation turns to spouse bashing, we stay silent or say something good about the other. This often causes enough discomfort in others to shift the conversation to a new topic.

We never open mail addressed specifically to the other, without permission. When I am at home and Rita receives an invitation or a report from a physical exam, I don't open it unless she is talking to me on her way home from work and asks me to do so. She does the same for me.

Both of us are pretty good at suppressing our anger or disgust with a situation when we are with other people. We give each other the gift of relaxing and letting it all hang out when it is just the two of us. It is a relief to be able to vent when my students have given me a bad time and I can say things that I wouldn't want anyone else to hear.

Sometimes we spend time with the other, even though we aren't really interested. Rita goes with me to college department parties, although she hardly knows anyone there. She has even gone to the auto show with me. I sometimes go shopping with her, sit with her when she gets her nails done and give her time to shop for shoes.

Other little things that Rita has done to make me feel special:

* When we eat out we sometimes have a single dessert for the two of us. Rita usually lets me have the last bite. Even when I tell her she can have it, she tells me she is finished so I will get that last bite.

* I usually get the garbage and recycling ready to go out to the curb for pickup. Sometimes, when we have been housecleaning or are cleaning up from a project, she comes out to the garage to help me.

* I am perfectly capable of ironing my own clothes, but sometimes I am slow to get to it and Rita will iron my clothes for me.

❋   As the kids were growing up, they often asked Rita to do an activity or buy something. She made them wait until I could be a part of the decision. The payoff for this came when our daughter got married. She and Rita went shopping for her wedding gown. When they found the dress, she insisted that I should be part of the decision. They called me from the bridal shop and waited until I got there to see her in it. She was stunning and I was overwhelmed to be included in the moment.

❋   I like to be well dressed but I don't get very excited about shopping for clothes for myself. Rita often goes shopping and purchases clothes for me. She brings them home and lets me look at and try them on. If I don't like them or they don't fit she takes them back.

❋   When we were teaching together, Rita often stopped in my classroom between classes just to check in and see how my day was going.

❋   Sometimes when the alarm goes off Rita moves over and snuggles for a couple of minutes before getting up.

❋   I like all kinds of electronic gadgets. Rita sometimes buys me gifts of electronics that I wouldn't buy for myself because I think they are too expensive.

❋ Rita gave me the book "Great Expectations" as a message that I should expect great things of our marriage and as permission to push her in that direction.

❋ Since I don't care much for cake, Rita sees to it that I get my favorite dessert, rhubarb pie, for my birthday.

❋ When I am working on a project around the house, she encourages me to buy a new tool that makes the job easier or allows me to produce a better result.

❋ I listen to a variety of music, including quite a bit of jazz. Rita doesn't care much for jazz, but when we travel she will include a little jazz to play in the car, because she knows I like it.

❋ Some men leave decorating the interior of the house to their wives and their wives consider it their domain. I am interested in the design and decoration of our house and she never makes a decision without including me.

Rita

Among the little things we do for each other, some require more time and effort than others. To illustrate the point, one of the things Bob did for me was to teach me to drive. I'm not exactly sure why I didn't have a driver's license when we got married. It is likely a combination of not being able to fit driver's education into my high school schedule, being in a family that only had one car and being the youngest and therefore not being very high on the usage list. After we had been married a few years, Bob found it more and more difficult to juggle his schedule to get me everywhere I needed to be so we decided it was time I learn to drive. He took the time and showed great patience as he taught me to drive. I trusted him and listened to everything he said. In fact, I listened so well to what he said and not exactly what the law said and failed the driver's test the first time I took it. But he took me back the second time and I got my license. He is never very comfortable being anywhere but in the drivers seat, so for years when we traveled, he would instantly go to sleep when I drove. I still don't care a lot about driving but I get myself to school, shopping and drive parts of trips when we travel. As the years have passed and as he has become comfortable with my driving, he no longer sleeps as often. Instead we talk and listen to music the same way we do when he drives. Being able to drive has definitely added to the quality of my life. While somebody else could have taught me, he took the time to do so. Interestingly enough, I did most of the practice driving with our children. In my mind, it is a clear demonstration of his love for and trust in me.

Bob loves gadgets, electronics and technology. He likes to take things apart and put them back together. It is not uncommon for me to come home to find that he has taken something apart, like my sewing machine, and is putting it back together so that it will work better and faster. I, on the other hand, just want things to do for me what they are designed to do. While I see him frustrated and hear strong words as he makes one more trip to the store, I consider it a great honor and act of love when he deals with me and computers. Most people who know me think one of my better qualities is patience. For whatever reason, computers try my patience. This is especially true when it is late at night and nothing seems to work the way it is supposed to, the computer crashes or I have forgotten to save the test that took me hours to create. I have been known to become irrational. While I know at some of those times Bob has wanted to say or do something to affirm my stupidity, he always stops what he's doing and comes to my rescue. On occasion he sends me to bed assuring me that he will fix it, and when I get up in the morning, I find all the papers I need for that day on my briefcase. He has even used his technology to fax a test to me at school when I have left it on the printer at home. When we worked together it got even better, he readily helped me during the passing period between classes or during his free period.

While the previous two examples might be "bigger" little things, there have been numerous little things that Bob has done or continues to do for me that let me know that I am special in his life.

* As part of a kitchen updating, we got new kitchen furniture and agreed that it was probably time to have dishes and glassware that match and aren't plastic. We agreed not to use the new tableware until the furniture arrived. When I came home the day the furniture was delivered, the table was set with all the new items on display complete with placemats, napkins and candles.

❀   I operate under the assumption that a person can't have too many friends or shoes. I like having shoes for every occasion. He indulges my need to have just one extra pair when we travel by offering to put a pair in his suitcase if necessary. When we installed a closet system, he took special care to make sure there was ample and designated space for all my shoes, even adding another shelf later. When we are out on one of our shopping adventures, he gives me ample time to browse the shoe stores and willingly makes an extra trip to the car if I've bought several pairs.

❀   I like roses and they have always been part of our relationship together. I receive them on various occasions, not always when expected. In addition, there has been a place in every house in which we have lived where he grows roses for me.

❀   While he is a "gadget freak" and dreams about the next electronic toy he can have, I was the first to have a cell phone and a laptop computer. He wanted me to be safe when I traveled alone at night and make my life easier when doing things for my classes.

❀   From the time I was a little girl I liked wearing simple jewelry. He has bought me jewelry many times through the years. Some of the jewelry has been expensive like the various gemstones I have. Others have been fun and thoughtful such as the Christmas he gave me a watch and ring to wear every day of the week. When I leave for work much earlier than he, he is willing to sit up in bed to help me put on a necklace or bracelet because I can't work the clasp.

* After many years of dreaming for a certain luxury car, Bob was able to purchase that car for himself. I never thought there was any difference in how cars drove. I used to say, "Just get me a roller skate with an engine." When we took his new car on a vacation trip I learned it did drive differently on interstate highways. A few years later, after he had finished a major consulting job, he bought a duplicate of that luxury car, for me.

* I don't like the way certain things feel. While fingernails on a chalkboard don't bother me, pulling cotton out of a medicine bottle or touching a peach gives me the creeps. So he pulls the cotton out of bottles and peels peaches for me so I can enjoy them.

* He finds it easy to compliment me on the way I dress and what I do. I find it mildly embarrassing but I know how much he cares about me when others talk about how wonderful of a person I am and he readily agrees with them.

❋ Bob always puts me first in front of others. He has a habit of kissing me first if we've been apart before he greets others. When the kids were little, they'd hang off his legs as he made his way to greet me first. Then he would pick them up and give each of them kisses and hugs.

Hints, Tips and Things We Learned Along the Way

* Small acts of kindness and caring add much to a relationship. They help us to feel loved and do much to keep us close. Many times we do them without really thinking about it. At times in our marriage we have set ourselves a goal to watch for an opportunity. It can be fun to find something special and do it when your spouse has no idea what you are up to.

* It is not good to get into comparing yourself with your spouse or anyone else in the little things that you do. Competition in this situation is destructive.

* Avoid developing expectations for the future when your spouse does something for you. In addition, little things should not be done with the expectation of a favor or gift in return.

* Do things as opportunities arise, but make a special effort occasionally. The element of surprise makes it special.

* Doing things for your spouse does not have to involve a financial commitment. It can be in the form of words of encouragement, time for themselves or taking care of some small task that they don't expect you to do.

❋   Some couples we know like to buy their
    spouse's Christmas gift first as a sign that they
    are number one.   We like to finish all the
    other shopping and then spend a day shopping
    for each other. Do whatever works for you.

❋   If you think you don't often do little things for
    each other, decide to spend a week trying to
    use any opportunity that arises. At the end of
    the week share your feelings about the effect
    of this on your relationship.

Questions to Help Guide Your Discussion/ Dialogue

Remember to share the feelings that go with the memories.

1. Where did I find me/us in Bob and Rita's story?

2. What importance do I place on the little things you do for me?

3. What five things you have done or that you do for me made/make me feel special?

4. How aware am I of little things I can do to make you feel special?

5. What motivates me to do little things for you?

EXPECTATIONS

"…they vote in Chicago – early and often." — Bob

"If I die tonight, promise me…" — Rita

Bob

In our interactions with others, we have expectations. I believe that I will behave in certain ways and the other person will also behave in certain ways. When Rita and I were married, I expected that we would have children and that she would stay home to care for them while I was the breadwinner of the family. I don't know that we ever had a discussion about that, but I would have been amazed if Rita had suddenly decided that she wanted to keep working after our first child was born. Fortunately, in this case, Rita's expectation matched mine and we did what we both expected to do.

It is not unusual for husbands and wives to have different expectations in many areas of their lives. One of the great sources of tension in a marriage is a mismatch between a husband's expectations of his wife and the reality of her

actual behavior and vice versa. The tension can only be resolved by adjusting one's expectations or changing the reality,
when that can be done.

We talked a lot about sex before we were married. We
were both interested and looking forward to it. I expected
that Rita would always be ready when I was and that we would
do it the way they vote in Chicago – early and often. That's
the way it went for a few weeks, then Rita started teaching
and suddenly, even though she was still interested, she was
tired at night and fell asleep early. I was in graduate school
and my schedule tended to be later than hers. I also needed
less sleep. Reality no longer matched my expectations. This
caused some tension between us, but I eventually learned to
adjust my expectations to be closer to reality.

A similar situation recurred in our marriage every time
a child was born. The demands of nursing and caring for a
newborn took their toll on Rita and sometimes on me. When
we recognized the differences in our expectations and talked
about them, she made an effort to give me a little more and
I tried to ask for a little less from her. In this situation, we
were able to make some adjustments in both our expectations
and the reality in which we were living. In our lives we never
seem to find an exact match between our expectations and
reality. It is worth the effort to try and then we learn to live
with the lower tension that remains.

When Rita went back to teaching after twenty years at
home with kids, we recognized that she would have less time
to take care of the children and the house and that I would
have to pick up some of the things she had been doing. By this
time we were aware of the importance of our expectations
and recognized that it would take multiple discussions over
time to work this out. I started to do more of the cooking

and often did the grocery shopping. I also made more effort to get to things like kids' soccer games when she was busy at school. At first, doing cooking and shopping seemed like intrusions on my time, but I agreed with Rita that it was necessary and eventually adjusted my schedule to accommodate the extra demands on me. After I retired, I picked up even more of the household work and sometimes did the laundry, which Rita had always done.

When I went back to full-time teaching, I knew that it would be more difficult to maintain my exercise schedule but I expected that we could find a way. Through the year, I found myself backing away from that expectation, but I didn't give it up. As we went into each year I continued to hope that we could maintain the exercise schedule we have in the summer. I am mindful that more discussions and compromises lie ahead.

Expectations aren't just associated with the activities of our lives. We also expect certain things in our personal interactions. In any situation I am usually an optimist, I look at things from the bright side and expect that the resolution will be favorable. For example, if I have a disagreement with a colleague, I tend to assume that it is over and that in the future, life will go on as before. In that kind of situation, Rita is more likely to worry and fret about her relationship with the colleague until she has some reassurance that the disagreement has been resolved. Even after forty years, I want her to respond in the same way I do and I become annoyed with her when I see what I interpret as her negative response. I would like to convince her that she should look at the bright side. I know that I cannot expect her response to be the same as mine and have learned to avoid making an issue of it.

As a result of our many discussions, the word "expectations" has become an important word in our vocabulary. On a Saturday morning it is not unusual for Rita to say to me, "What's the POA—Plan of Action? What are your expectations for today?" It opens a discussion that allows me to be frank about the things I intend to do or need to get done that day and allows her to let me know her plans. We work out the schedule of our day together and avoid assumptions and expectations that could turn out to be wrong and lead to more stress in our lives.

Rita

We all have expectations of ourselves and others. It is impossible to be in a relationship without them. The problem is trying to match expectations with reality. While I didn't name them, I'm sure I brought many expectations to our marriage. I expected that we would live happily ever after; that no matter what the situation we faced, we would be able to handle it. I likely expected that neither of us would change so that there would never be any problems in our lives. Most importantly, I'm sure I expected Bob to meet all the expectations I had of him and fill all my needs. I could go on and on, but the reality is many of the expectations I had weren't real. First of all, in order for an expectation to be met, both people in a relationship have to know the expectation is there. Much of what we have written in the following chapters has to do with expectations and what we assumed each of us would or would not do. As we were discussing this chapter before we put it on paper, we saw the correlation between expectations and reality and the playfulness in our relationship. I sat down on a pool chair to talk with Bob about what we were going to write. My elbow fell through a hole in the webbing. I said that I had expected the chair to support me, but in reality the webbing was broken. We laughed as we talked about expectations and reality and suddenly every trivial thing we did the next few minutes was somehow tied to those two things. While this example may not seem profound, the realization of the link between the two is very important. We have learned that each of us must recognize and state the expectations we have of ourselves and the other in real situations. If our expectations can't be met, experience has shown us that the expectations may be unrealistic and need to be changed. The following is an example that supports this.

I am a very organized person and have a need for order in all aspects of my life. I see this as very freeing and it enables me to do a variety of things, have many projects going at one time, make others comfortable and do most things I need to complete on time. My cabinets and closets are neatly organized. Laundry is folded to fit the space in which it is stored. When our children were small, I made sure that all the puzzle pieces and parts to a toy were put where they belonged. I leave my desk neat at the end of each day. I make a mental list of what I need to accomplish each day while showering in the morning. I know the number of things I want to do and keep track of what I've done. Post-it notes are my friend. At home, I generally know where things are since my philosophy is that everything has a place and everything should be put in its place. I'm not a fanatic and I can go to bed at the end of a busy day without having everything cleaned up and put away. But I have said as we crawl into bed, "If I die tonight, promise me you'll clean up before you let people in our house."

Bob in general is very neat and tidy so my expectations in this area are most often met. However, there are two areas of our house, the den and his garage workshop, that

I pretty much leave alone, especially his desk and workbench. While I encourage and often help with the organization, I never organize either of them without his being present and part of the project. While he knows that I like everything in its place, it is just something he never quite gets around to doing. About once a year we set aside time to put away the tools and file or throw things out in the den. I have learned to accept that it is unrealistic of me to expect that he will keep it that way. We laugh about how long the organization will last. I've accepted that the time of the organization is on his schedule, not mine. The reality for me is that his den will never be as organized as I would like. The most important thing is that I have learned to live with that. Accepting this has reduced stress and tension between us. We have merely closed the door on occasion when we have guests and he straightens it up when we've needed to use the den for a guest bedroom. We've come to accept that whenever I've been in the room, I will likely put one thing away and close the closet doors on my way out.

On the other hand, expectations have helped me to grow as a person. It is one of the reasons I gave Bob the book, Great Expectations. Going back to when we were married, even though I wanted to be a teacher and had a college degree, I expected that when we had children I would be a stay at home mom. But as I wrote in the chapter, "When Dreams Come True", even my own expectations can become difficult when I try to live them out. While I would not have changed being home the years that I was, there were moments when I missed adult companionship, the intellectual challenge of being in the classroom and just being in a world larger than our house. The challenge for me was to find ways to use the gifts that I had rather than what I expected. I volunteered in our children's schools and in our parish. When we were in leadership positions in the Marriage Encounter organization, I learned some important things about myself and my abilities that I now use in my teaching career. Having to deal with reality and not what we expected hasn't been all bad. What I am trying to learn now is what real expectations I should have of myself and our life together as we age and when we no longer have a career per se. I will continue to have expectations, but I will have to accept the reality that aging will demand.

Hints, Tips and Things We Learned Along the Way

❋   Expectations are okay. No matter how hard couples try to avoid them, expectations sneak into every marriage. Unmet expectations are frequently the 800 pound gorilla that people try to ignore. The key to growth in your relationship is to recognize that some will never be met, some will be more than met and some will need to be adjusted along the way.

❋   Tension in a relationship likely indicates that expectations are not being met. A discussion about the expectations you have in the area causing the stress allows you to voice them and make adjustments if and where necessary.

❋   Remember that the only person you can change or expect to change is you. Expecting the other person to change or thinking that you can change them may lead to greater disappointment, stress and unresolved arguments. Change may be necessary, but it must be chosen freely, not demanded.

❋   Since expectations are individual and change often, you will need to constantly state and restate the expectations you have of one another. Friends of ours wanted to try new things in their sexual relationship. They had many discussions with us about possibilities.

One day she came home from work to find every mirror in their house in their bedroom. This didn't fit her expectations. Had they been more specific with each other, they likely could have avoided the big fight that resulted.

❋ Children, families, friends, jobs, commitments, etc., all place expectations on you. Expectations in these areas must be identified and re-identified as time passes. Sometimes, for the sake of your relationship, you may have to make a decision not to meet the expectations of others. The key is to talk about how you are going to be able to live with the decisions you make.

❋ Since everyone changes and situations change, there is never a perfect plan or ultimate solution. You can never fully resolve the differences in your expectations and that will likely leave some tension in your relationship. The key is to have on-going discussions and find a level of tension that you can live with. We still live with some differences in how we approach our finances, but knowing those differences allows us to manage the tension in a healthy way.

❋ Holidays have their way of creating expectations. Sometimes the card, the gift, the special dinner just doesn't happen or doesn't meet the expectation. It is important to have realistic expectations in this area. But, it is more important to enjoy and appreciate the fact that your spouse thought about you and cared enough to do what they did.

* Because you want to strengthen the relationship you have, avoid making judgments about the other's expectations. While some expectations may be unrealistic, on-going discussions will help each of you be more realistic.

Questions to Help Guide Your Discussion/ Dialogue

Remember to share your feelings along with your thoughts and opinions. Some of the responses may bring up difficult feelings. Keep in mind that the goal is to have a loving discussion, not to prove that the other needs to change.

1. Where did I find me/us in Bob and Rita's story?

2. How do I think expectations affect our relationship? Give examples of this.

3. A time when you most fully met my expectation/s was...

4. A time when you did not meet my expectation/s was...

5. In what area of our relationship do you most often meet my expectation/s?

6. In what area of our relationship do you most often not meet my expectation/s?

7. How do I behave toward you when you don't meet my expectations?

8. In what area of our relationship do I think I need to revisit my expectations?

9. When you can identify tension in your relationship, consider the following question. Where are my expectations about _____ _____ not being met?

KEEPING THE DREAM ALIVE

"… two eyes that watched her…" — Bob

"…door handles and … antenna." — Rita

Bob

Probably our most compelling reason for getting married was the element of being "in love" that we hoped would last for a lifetime. I thought that Rita was wonderful. She listened to me and I looked forward to sharing everything with her. There was a playfulness and tenderness in our relationship that people associate with young lovers. We expected to go through our lives holding hands as we shopped and laughing as we had water fights with the hose. I looked forward to Rita always laughing at my dumb jokes and expected that I would want to hear how she would decorate a room in our home. There was a sexual tension between us that added to the fun of being together. We had heard about the romance eventually going away and that we would have to "settle down," but we didn't think that would happen to us. In fact, we were sure that our dream for us was too big to let that happen.

As the years passed, we experienced the pressures to "settle down" and sometimes they pushed the "in love" part of our marriage into the background for a while. We never let that part of our relationship get suppressed too much and made efforts along the way to keep our romantic dreams alive.

In the early, days almost everything we did had an aura of romance. Cooking meals and eating together, waking up with Rita next to me, shopping for groceries for us and buying a gift for Christmas or Rita's birthday were all things that seemed romantic and special.

I learned something about romance from my parents. There was not a lot of money and there were many children, so their spending on each other was limited. It seemed that every Christmas Eve my dad would disappear for a little while and no one in the family knew where he had gone. When he returned, he had a gift for my mother. Each year it was a gift she had expressed wanting but wouldn't buy herself.

My mother saved dimes through the year and used them to buy a gift for my father. One year it was a new suit. She wanted him to look good when he dressed up. While the gifts they bought were often practical and may not have seemed romantic, they were one of the ways they kept the spark alive in their marriage.

Romance has been part of our marriage from the beginning. The first or second Christmas of our married life, I spent a lot of time finding a beautiful long white bathrobe for Rita. It had a rose on the front and I knew that she would look great in it. It cost more than we had agreed to spend, but I had to have it. This started a pattern for my Christmas gifts for Rita. I almost always spend more than we agree we will spend on each other.

One year during Lent I decided that I needed to romance Rita more, so I committed to doing some special little thing for her each day. I didn't tell her what I was doing, so each day was a surprise. One of the things I remember best is making a banner which said: "I Love You!" and taping it to the shower doors in our bathroom. Inside the shower, I taped to the wall a piece of paper with two eyes that watched her while she showered.

A few years ago I had two short hospital stays. Rita took me to the hospital in the middle of the night the first time. The second time she got a call at school to come to the hospital. She visited me while trying to keep up with her classes and assured our children around the country that I would be okay. I thought she should be aware of how much her caring meant to me, so I had a dozen roses sent to her classroom with a "Thank you!" message. I wanted to surprise her and have her students see the flowers so she would have to explain their appearance.

An enduring element of our lives together is my constant awareness of how much Rita loves me. She has a look for me that plays an important role in this. Every so often she snuggles against my chest and looks up at me with love in her eyes that melts me inside. It happens when we are alone and when we are in public. It catches me by surprise and while the periods in between may be long, I can bask in that look for a long time!

We like to have fun together – we call it playfulness – over little things. Some of these situations happen once and we have a laugh together or tease a little before going on, while others have been part of our lives since the beginning of our relationship. These fun times involve gentle teasing and help us to laugh at ourselves with each other. They are done with great affection.

Rita has a special little giggle that tells me she finds something funny. Usually I don't know what it is, but I expect to be entertained and I can't wait to find out. I don't know whether anyone else is aware of it, but it is one of the things that endears her to me.

When we were home from our honeymoon for only a few days, Rita came out of the shower and I took the opportunity to snap a towel at her bottom. She surprised me by yelling: "Wife beater!" It was August and the windows were open as were the windows of nearby apartments. I found myself suddenly embarrassed and insisted that Rita be quiet. We ended up laughing about it then and continue to laugh about it today.

Years later I turned the tables on Rita. We were grocery shopping in the produce section in the middle of the afternoon. I sneaked up behind her, propositioned her and made suggestive remarks. She was red with embarrassment and kept looking around to be sure no one else could hear as she tried to get me to stop. I continue to surprise her with this when we shop. She has gotten better, but it still makes her uncomfortable, even while she is laughing with me. She has retaliated by calling me a "Dirty Old Man." My response, of course, is that she would be disappointed if I weren't.

When I want to know the condition of our relationship, I look at the state of our playfulness with each other. If we are teasing, goofing around and frequently engaged in playful activities, I know we are in good shape. When there is tension between us, these same activities are annoying and

I don't consider trying them. Frequent affectionate teasing is a reliable indicator to me that we are in a good place with each other.

Spending time together is important to us. In the beginning, we had very little money, so we tended to do inexpensive things. We would window shop or browse through a bookstore or furniture shop. In the browsing and talking about the things we saw, we learned a good bit about each other's likes and dislikes. Going to Saturday afternoon Mass in the Cathedral in Cincinnati was a way to be together and acknowledged that our Catholic faith was an important part of our lives. We still do those inexpensive things and have added touring model homes – sometimes because we are looking, but more often just to see what is there and to get decorating ideas. It gives us time to talk about many things and relax together.

Of course, now that we have a bigger budget, we sometimes spend some money, too. When Rita and I went on an exercise program, we both lost enough weight to need new wardrobes. While I like to be well dressed, I am never very sure about my fashion sense. I enjoy having Rita shop with me and help me to find clothes that we both like on me. She trusts me to help her make decisions about the color or fit of clothes that she purchases for herself. We laugh at the disasters that looked good on the rack but not on us.

In our travels, we may spend a day on the beach reading books. We don't talk a lot, but it's nice to know that we can. We take a break once in a while to get into the water and chat for a time before going back to our books. In recent years, we have chosen some of our travel destinations as possible places to retire. While there, we look around the area and get some ideas about its suitability to us. We have fun describing for each other how we see living there or laughing at decorator schemes that are not in our style.

Rita

There has always been a kind of "tenderness" in our relationship that indicates that we care about each other. It puts flesh on the words, "I love you," which we say each day. Looking back, it started with the candies he dropped on my desk in high school and the wild roses he picked on his way to one of our dates. He has a glint in his eyes that is meant only for me. It can happen whether we are across the table from each other or across a crowded room. When we taught together he would casually appear in the hallway outside my classroom. When I saw that glint in his eye, my heart would skip a beat like it did when we were in high school and I found it difficult to concentrate on the lesson. It happened when he came into my classroom or we walked down the hallway together. Even students noticed and some adults made comments. No one else brightens my life in the way he does. Keeping this tenderness and attraction in our relationship is important. I don't know whether this happens because of the closeness we have or if it sustains the closeness. I don't suppose it matters which, but I do know that it is an essential part of who we are and what our marriage is.

In this tenderness, there is a hint of more or a promise that this will continue in the things that I do. When we were dating, it was in the letters we wrote to each other. The urgency to be together was in every one. I still have the last one he wrote to me tucked in a cookbook and periodically I read it. It helps me to remember how much we wanted to be together. Even though we wrote to each other every day for 25 years, that wasn't always enough to convey what I felt.

When Bob taught at the community college I would send him greeting cards at school. Sometimes they just told him how much I cared and others gave him a hint of what to expect when he came home. The secretaries commented about the expression on his face when he opened them. In the years he was home, I left them on his computer keyboard or on the breakfast table when I left for school. They were simple reminders to him that I would not forget him that day no matter how busy I was. Teaching together let me put cards in his mailbox or send a quick email.

Some of the activities are more fun and require a little planning. I got the idea to fill his office with balloons, but since I couldn't figure out how to get the key, I decided to fill his car instead. The kids and I blew up hundreds of balloons and stuffed his car with them as it sat in the parking lot. We tied them to the door handles and to the antenna. They streamed out of the car as he opened the door. There were balloons in his car for many days to follow. When we are trying to deal with the realities of life, doing things like this helps us to remember why we want to live together forever.

Playfulness in our relationship is as important for me as it is Bob. It reminds me that I am still young at heart. It occurs with some gifts on special occasions that come with a twist of humor. In addition to the other gifts I got him one Christmas; I put together little items that honor the three things he likes to do most. First, he is very mechanical and handy so I got him a screwdriver. Secondly, Bob enjoys an occasional alcoholic beverage so I gave him a corkscrew. Thirdly, to honor the physical aspect of our relationship that he enjoys a lot, I gave him—well; I won't tell you what I gave him!

This playfulness seems to be part of everything we do, whether we are talking about an area of our relationship, shopping at the supermarket or mall or singing along to goofy songs on the car stereo as we travel. It continues to remind us that not everything in life needs to be serious. The ability to laugh at ourselves allows us to relieve tension and settle some potential conflicts before they actually hurt one of us.

On a trip, I found myself needing to use every rest area and sometimes something else in between. We were late getting started on the trip and the plan was to travel a good distance yet that first day, so I was concerned that all the stops would hamper our travel schedule. After we made several stops, I jokingly referred to myself as the "pee queen." After we laughed about my remark, I asked Bob if he was stressed by the number of stops we were making. He replied with a "no" and said it was probably better for both of us to get out of the car more often and another hour in the car that day or the next didn't really matter. We still managed to get to our original destination at a reasonable hour.

We genuinely like each other and do consider each other our best friend. As all good friends do, we have inside jokes and funny activities that we engage in together. This began in part with my calling Bob "Yogi." Through the years, it has developed more. I've gotten into a hit and run activity when Bob is in the shower. He is happily showering himself, totally unaware that I am in the room, and I bomb him with a big container of cold water and then run out of the room, usually before he figures out what happened. Bob has jokingly said that he doesn't get mad, he gets even, so after biding his time and he thinks I have forgotten, the same thing happens to me. We have on occasion made a mess in our bathroom that we would not have tolerated from our children. But it's fun.

Bob loves cars almost as much as computers or maybe it's the other way around. He is always looking at the newest and latest model. This is something that he shares with our sons. At family gatherings, the women roll their eyes as the conversation changes from one to the other and back again. As the years have passed and something hasn't gone the way that I perceive Bob or I expected, I tell Bob that he ought to trade me in on a new model, someone with more power, pizzazz and speed. Bob's usual response is, "What would I do with a new model? I'd have to break in a new model and who wants to do that? I'm comfortable with this one and who'd want me anyway?" It's just our way of letting each other know, that in spite of things not going the way we expected, there is no one else we'd rather spend our life with.

Friendship, nurturing and caring for it, is important in any relationship. Friendships drift into acquaintances or fond memories without attention and time spent together. To maintain the level of closeness and intimacy that we want, Bob and I try to spend time together. It doesn't mean we have to be joined at the hip. He can go to the home improvement store by himself, but if I've had a very busy week and haven't seen much of him, I might go along for the ride and we can chat as he gets the things he needs. This began when the kids were little. It might have been more efficient if he'd gone alone, but we got the kids ready and all went. It got me out of the house and we had some time together. The kids didn't mind and we had some interesting conversations with them as well.

We are fortunate in having similar tastes in many things. We know many couples who could not be more opposite and have to learn the art of compromise more comprehensively than we have. We both like to read. Some authors we share in common, but when I'm reading my favorite historical romance, Bob usually isn't interested or if he's reading a spy thriller, I don't look at it as a book I'd like to read. Through the years I have read a few thrillers and he has even read a few romance novels. Even when we aren't interested in the author, we stop and ask each other to tell what's happening in our book. It is sort of like reading two books at once.

Since we're always interested in the future, we never end one vacation without having some idea where we'd like to go next. It was fun when we were camping with the kids, letting them talk about where they'd like to go next, and it continues now that we are on our own. Some vacation opportunities have just presented themselves without our planning, like the trip to South Africa with friends, but we have a list of places we'd like to see together. The most exotic at the moment is a trip to Tahiti. Planning for and looking forward to the next vacation helps us to keep the dream alive.

Hints, Tips and Things We Learned Along the Way

* Keeping a relationship strong requires spending time together. If your relationship is to have priority, you may have to reevaluate the amount of time you spend with friends or on your job. It is possible to do your job well, enjoy friendships and have a great marriage, too, but it requires constant attention and effort or the situation will become unbalanced. Sometimes we tolerate a temporary imbalance. The end of every school year seems to be very busy for us and our time together is usually reduced for a couple of weeks, but we are careful not to let it become a permanent or long-term situation.

* When priorities are out of balance there are always options, although sometimes the best option for your marriage may require a difficult decision.

* You are never too old for romance and playfulness. There is an attitude in our society that marriage is for settling down. A young man should sow his wild oats. A young woman should travel with her girl friends. When they get married, the fun will end and they will have to settle down. We have asked teenagers about this and many of them think grown ups never have fun. They see adult lives as

too serious and they don't want to grow up. We think that some of the "fun" things that people do are wasted on the young. Rita has no regrets about never vacationing with the girls. The early vacations we took together were part of the friendship building we needed. When Rita was seven months pregnant we climbed to the top of Clingman's Dome in the Smokey Mountains. We still laugh about the comments people made especially the woman who said, "If that pregnant woman can do it, so can I." You can find ways to have fun and romance each other, no matter how many years you are married.

* People tend to romance their spouse the way they like to be romanced. Think about what your spouse likes and what will make him or her feel special. A couple we know were invited to a family wedding in San Francisco. While her first reaction was to fly, especially with two young children, she thought about how much her husband liked trains. So instead they took the train from Chicago to San Francisco and back.

* Some attempts at playfulness may fail. When Rita was pregnant at Christmas and feeling depressed, I bought her a little plastic figure of a fat guy. On the base it said, "I love you just the way you are!" I was trying to reassure Rita of my love, but she did not find it funny!

Your relationship will survive a disaster or two, so keep trying.

* Most relationships are enhanced by the element of surprise. Romantic things may be expected on birthdays and anniversaries, but don't limit yourself to those times.

* Some situations require serious responses, but developing a sense of playfulness in your marriage can help to turn situations that could lead to tension into times when you laugh at yourselves instead.

* Romantic and playful activities don't necessarily lead to sex.

* It is OK to be romantic and playful in front of your children. It is one of the best ways to teach them how to be married.

Questions to Help Guide Your Discussion/ Dialogue

Remember to share the feelings that go with the memories.

1. Where do I see me/us in Bob and Rita's story?

2. How important do I think romance and playfulness are in our relationship?

3. Do I think we romance each other enough?

4. Am I satisfied with the level of playfulness in our marriage?

5. Describe a time when you romanced me.

6. Remember a time when we were playful together and talk about it.

7. Share something you do that lets me know you love me.

8. Describe a time when I was pleasantly surprised by something you did for me.

9. Share something we haven't done that I think would be romantic.

10. When you have finished this discussion each plan a time and an activity to romance the other. Make it a surprise!

MAKING DECISIONS AND RESOLVING DIFFERENCES

"…she obviously couldn't hear me…" — Bob

"it's your fault." — Rita

Bob

I grew up in a family that didn't often fight. I got into a tussle with my sisters occasionally, but my parents didn't tolerate much yelling or name-calling. I'm not sure how my parents resolved their differences. I knew they sometimes had differences – I could hear the tension in their voices, but I never heard them yell at each other. I suspect that in many cases, my father made the final decision and my mother let him have his way.

I know almost nothing about the way my uncles and aunts related to each other, but I was always fascinated when my dad and my uncles would get together. They often had rather loud and intense arguments about a variety of subjects.

I don't know why I remember this, but one Sunday afternoon at our house, it was about organic farming. You would think they were having quite a fight, but after listening for a while you would notice that everybody had changed sides and the argument was going on as strongly as ever. They were enjoying the exercise of arguing.

I have some tendency to get into the same kind of arguments and our children have learned to jump right in. Sometimes it gets rather loud and intense. Rita has never been comfortable with this and sometimes intervenes to get us to stop. This pastime also causes discomfort for some of our in-law children and they have been known to move to a different part of the house to get away from us. I guess you have to grow up with it.

I don't remember having very many differences with Rita during our dating years. We were apart most of the time and when we were together, we didn't want to waste our time on disagreements. I can't even recall any big disagreements in the process of planning our wedding.

Rita and I have never been fighters who yell or throw things. At worst, I would describe our disagreements as heated discussions and even those are pretty rare. From the beginning of our marriage, Rita rarely got upset enough about anything to start a heated discussion. She seemed to take everything as it came. If she was upset about something she remained silent. When tension arose, it always seemed to me that I was the one who was tense, so I was the one who started the discussion.

I am a problem-solver. Whatever I do, I have a need to understand everything about the situation. I want to make my best decision and have arguments ready to defend it if questioned. I can often analyze a situation quickly so that it doesn't take long to marshal my reasons. This works well when I'm buying a car. I'm competitive, and in a political argument, become intense about winning. I avoid video games because I get so involved that they frustrate me.

I tended to approach any difference between us as another problem to be solved. I wouldn't bring up an issue with Rita until all my arguments were prepared. I was mostly focused on getting the outcome I had already decided was best. In the process I lost my sense of caring for Rita. If she questioned me or presented her side of the issue, I was ready with my counter-argument. Rita says that as I responded to her with my arguments, my voice would get louder and louder. I say that if she disagreed with me, she obviously couldn't hear me at my current level. Having my arguments at hand and speaking them loudly was my way of controlling the discussion. No matter what she said, I had an answer and often it was one that I had given some thought. She was left trying to catch up and respond on the spur of the moment. She often responded by saying, "I'm sorry!" That left me frustrated and angry. I wanted to resolve the issue between us and this didn't do it. She hadn't even admitted that I was right and the tension often remained.

As I was growing up I was always at the top of my class, but definitely never in the group of most popular kids. When they were choosing sides for a softball or basketball game, I was one of the last to be picked. At the same time, people liked it when I was able to solve their problems for them. I came to believe that people liked me for my ability to solve their problems, but didn't really like the person I was.

Over the years with each other I discovered that Rita's love for me didn't depend on my ability to solve problems for her. Eventually we had a discussion about the negative effect of my problem-solving approach and aggressive defense of my decisions. Since that discussion, I have tried to be more open to Rita's ideas and to be sure that she has input. Often she has a suggestion that is better than mine and I am happy to go with it. Even when I think my idea is better, I find myself saying, "Have you considered this?" instead of, "I have a better way." I try to respect her ideas and not respond with a put-down. The control that I once tried so hard to maintain now seems unnecessary. Rita provides more input and our discussions tend to be more productive.

We have discovered that tension in our relationship is often associated with the way we make decisions. Sometimes the issue is whether one of us has made the right decision. At other times a big issue is our differing perceptions about when a decision has been made or even whether a decision has been made.

We have always had discussions about decisions, especially the big ones. I tend to be slow to make decisions. When we consider buying a car or a house, I want to be sure that I have all the information and have considered all the options. This often takes time and I am not sure when I will come to the end of the process. A source of tension in the decision-making process is that Rita doesn't share my hesitation.

One day we were in an auto dealer's showroom while our car was being repaired. We looked at vehicles on the showroom floor, especially one model I hadn't seen before. I thought that it looked nice and could possibly be a replacement for my car. We talked about whether it was time to trade my car, while it still had some value, or keep it until it totally wore out. I certainly wanted to consider other vehicles before deciding on a replacement and hadn't decided whether to trade soon or in a couple of years. At that time

I didn't know how that car would have fit into our finances. Later in the day, Rita was talking to our son on the phone and I was surprised to hear her say, "Dad has found the car he wants next." While we had discussed the possibility that this could be my next car, from my point of view, I wasn't even car shopping. At most I considered this to be casual research.

When we plan a vacation and have made a decision about where we want to go, I usually do much of the searching for transportation and rental cars. Rita researches hotels but I tend to do the actual reservations. My desire to get the best arrangements at the best price often prompts me to delay the reservations today in hopes for a better deal tomorrow or the next day. Rita is ready to book the trip, but I wait. Sometimes she gets frustrated with my hesitation and says, "Let's just DO it!" The truth is that we have sometimes lost our best deal in waiting for a better one. I am learning from this and now try to book trips more quickly and just not worry about saving that last dollar.

I don't believe that our discussions on this subject have brought about any real changes in the way I make decisions. I've learned that I may want more time before I finalize a decision or time to get up the energy to jump into a project. When Rita pushes for a decision, she forces me to let her know where I stand. The benefit of knowing how each of us goes through the process keeps us aware of what is happening. This helps me to get past my hesitation and move more quickly.

Rita

Since my father died when I was nine, I have limited experience of how my parents made decisions and resolved whatever differences they had. I do know that I never heard them verbally argue. Occasionally, my father and older siblings had a heated verbal exchange. I don't think I ever heard my mother raise her voice to anyone. As my older siblings married and I spent time with them, I can't recall verbal outbursts in their relationships either. In general, I came from a relatively peaceful family. That doesn't mean there were not differences of opinions or differing views on various subjects. Everyone seemed to handle whatever differences they had in a reserved way. As a result, I brought to our marriage the expectations that when we were resolving differences, shouting and loud verbal discussions were not needed.

Like many adolescents, I was unsure of others' perception of me. I excelled in school and found that I was a confidant to many. Frequently, I fell into the roll of peacemaker and helped others resolve differences. This is something I still do today. Co-workers and sometimes total strangers ask me for advice. Experience has shown me that I am a good listener and can help others sort out issues in their lives. When we were married, I believed we were the one couple that could live happily ever after. While I didn't expect that we would face any major differences, at the very least I expected that I could peaceably resolve any differences we might have.

What attracted me to Bob was his ability to think things through and to express his thoughts and reasons very logically. Because of that, I saw myself and often still see myself as inferior to him and certainly not his equal when it comes to critical thinking and decision making. This was reinforced in disagreements we had. Bob countered anything that I had to say with what appeared to be logical reasons, and tension seemed to arise if I didn't accede to the rightness of his arguments. I concluded that his arguments were obviously better than mine and the discomfort we felt was my fault, not his. Being the peacemaker, I merely said, "I'm sorry," expecting that to settle the issue. When this didn't lessen the tension or added to it, I didn't know how to resolve the differences. My ideas were obviously not important or, at the very least, I was incapable of presenting them in a logical, well thought out way. Rather than spend my time and energy to do that, I merely deferred to Bob.

Looking back, these patterns of behaviors were there before we married; we just didn't recognize them. Some of my college friends and I decided to experiment with changing our hair color. I chose to add some red to my natural color. I thought it looked flattering and wrote about it in a letter to Bob. His response was, "Get the red out of your hair before I see you." Why he had that reaction is unimportant. He has no idea today why he reacted the way he did. What is important was my response. I washed my hair morning and night trying to get the color out. I wanted to please him and have things be peaceful when we got together. There were still vestiges of the red when I next saw him. I immediately told him I was sorry. I believed that he must have logical arguments even though I didn't comprehend them. The whole thing is funny today since we both have colored our natural gray.

Contrary to my perception, we did have different ideas on some issues that needed to be resolved. In the early years, we found ways, some more successful than others, to keep our relationship peaceful. In general, we did talk about everything. When we didn't totally agree, I let Bob make the final decision. It wasn't a bad way to live. I figured out ways to get my point across when I didn't think Bob was listening to me. I was either silent or made a quick point and changed the subject. That way there was no argument for him to counter or he had no time to do so. As our communication improved, we gained a better understanding of our interactions as we tried to make decisions. Bob described the anger he felt when I so easily said I was sorry. He wanted me to counter his arguments to help him rethink the issue. I told him the feelings of frustration and disappointment I felt when his louder arguments said to me that he found no value in what I had to say. Most importantly, we learned that neither of us needs to be right and neither needs to be a peacemaker. The objective in resolving disagreements is that both of us are heard and both believed that our input had value. The result is greater trust.

We discovered that we could reduce tension by figuring out the actual source of that tension. When I became aware of it, I learned to ask Bob if he was okay or what was bothering him. That led to a major breakthrough for me. While it happened over time, I began to believe that I was an equal partner in our discussions and in our relationship. I recognized that Bob, in fact, was listening to me. In discussions, he began to affirm me by commenting on the fact that I did, indeed, have good ideas and they made sense. I was helping him to see yet another dimension of a situation that he had not considered. I have gained more self-confidence and the stress that accompanies this has been reduced.

The playful aspect of our relationship has helped us here as well. How this developed I don't really know, but whenever anything little goes wrong over which Bob has no control, I say to him, "it's your fault." It might be as simple as it is raining outside and I want it to be sunny. He might not be in the same room and I stub my toe. I say it's his fault when he asks why I said, "Ouch!" He does the same. It may seem silly, but it helps us take the appropriate action when it is indeed our fault.

In addition to resolving differences, tension can occur from the very process by which each of us makes decisions. I think things through to the best of my ability, take an action and then live with the consequences. In making some decisions, I list all the pros and cons and then determine which outweighs the other. I decide to do what the process indicates. Whether it is the right or wrong decision in the end doesn't matter to me. I live with the consequences. In our marriage, when making a decision with Bob, I listen carefully to what he says. I try to hear all points that he has thought about. The cause of the stress between us in that process occurs when I perceive that after every possible scenario has been talked about and all the pros and cons have been evaluated, he is still indecisive. I don't think there is any more discussion to be had. In many cases I think the process has made the decision. When he comes back a few days later with more ideas or puts off taking the action I think we agreed to, I get frustrated. This guy who can solve everybody else's problem can't make a decision. I am better at recognizing my frustration and voicing it, but it is still in process. It takes repeated experiences to help us realize what we are doing.

We had been discussing for sometime the need for major improvements to our previous home. Four children had been or were being raised there, and after fifteen years, it certainly needed some updating. We talked about it and I thought we were in agreement. We both seemed excited with the plans we were making, had gathered information on a contractor, knew how we were going to finance it and had set a tentative time schedule. I thought the decision had been made but it seemed to me that the closer we got to the beginning of the project, the more hesitancy Bob had. I was frustrated and I didn't like my feelings when I talked with him about the plans. Earlier in our marriage I would have lived with this and kept silent, knowing we would eventually get to it when Bob got ready. With summer fast approaching and my time available to work on the project, I gathered my confidence one morning and simply said to him, "Are we going to do this or not? I want to do it but if you don't just, tell me. I don't want to spend any more time and energy planning it if we're not going to do it." It was still rare for me to directly confront an issue. He quickly responded by saying that we were indeed going to do it, and within a few weeks we began the project. As we later talked about this, I learned that when I think we have made a decision, there might just be one more thing that he hasn't considered that could potentially change the whole thing. Even if he thinks he has every aspect worked out, he still finds it a major decision to begin. Once he starts, he's okay. Today when we are in a decision making process, I ask, "Have we or have we not made a decision? If you're not ready to proceed, could you please tell me when you're ready to begin?" Then I can put my energy into other things. In addition, I have figured out that I can help him to bypass his hesitancy by a minor push—well, sometimes it requires a major push. We are both happier with the result.

Hints, Tips and Things We Learned Along the Way

* If one of you sees a problem in making decisions or resolving differences, there is a problem. The very existence of your difference in perception is a problem and it needs to be resolved.

* Mutually agree on a time to have your discussion. It gives both of you a chance to be emotionally prepared and avoids making the issue worse by forcing a discussion. However, avoiding the issue will not make it go away.

* Remember that you are trying to build your relationship. The following are things we and other couples have used when trying to resolve an issue:

  1. Know what the issue is and stick to it. The cause of conflict may not have anything to do with the two of you. Start by clarifying the cause.

  2. No past history. Our general rule is that any issue older than the milk in the refrigerator is no longer open for discussion.

  3. No name calling. Calling names belittles your spouse.

4. Few issues are black and white, so avoid absolutes. Don't use words like: "you always…" or "you never…" They are rarely true. Use words like "sometimes…" or "occasionally…" or "it seems to me…."

5. The discussion of the issue should be kept between the two of you. Keep family members, bosses and friends out of the discussion.

6. Stay in close physical contact. It's easier to stay focused on your relationship when you are near each other. You might even try holding hands.

7. Stay until the issue is resolved. Don't hit and run. Don't use tears as a weapon.

8. Look at your usual behavior in an argument and avoid those things that get in the way of resolving the issue.

9. Always fight for your relationship, not to prove that you are right.

❖ There are no quick fixes. Some issues may take several sessions to resolve. If your discussion seems to be stuck, you are just rehashing the same old stuff or one of you is too emotional, it may be time to set another date to try again.

❋ Listening is as important as speaking. Conflicts are much more readily resolved when you listen to each other with caring and love and with a genuine interest in what the other has to say.

❋ The message you hear in your spouse's words may not be the message your spouse is trying to convey. Make an effort to give and get feedback.

❋ Choose your battles. Not everything is worth fighting about. Decide to accept some things and focus on the important issues.

❋ Have a discussion on how each of you makes decisions. Knowing this can take the mystery out of patterns of behavior that don't seem to make sense.

Questions to Help Guide Your Discussion/ Dialogue

Remember to share your feelings about your response to each question.

Resolving Differences

1. Where did I find me/us in Bob and Rita's story?

2. How do I see us resolving differences? Is it constructive or destructive?

3. What were the strengths in the way my family resolved differences? How does that affect how we resolve them?

4. What were the weaknesses in the way my family resolved differences? How does that affect how we resolve them?

5. Which of the hints for resolving differences do I think we use well?

6. Which of the hints for resolving differences would I like to try?

7. What behavior of yours when we are resolving differences do I find most difficult to understand?

8. Is there something that would make it easier for us to resolve differences, if I would just let go? Am I willing to try to do so?

9. What change/s could we make to improve our ability to resolve differences? Am I willing to try to do so?

Making Decisions

1. What do I think are our strengths in the way we make decisions?

2. What do I think are the limitations of the way we make decisions?

3. Are we equal partners in decision making?

4. How did my family make decisions? How does that affect what we do?

5. What behavior of yours when we are making decisions do I find most difficult to understand?

6. When do I most enjoy making a decision/s with you?

7. What change/s could we make to improve our ability to make decisions? Am I willing to try to do so?

FORGIVENESS AND HEALING

"…I sacrificed my pride, my fears…" — Rita

"…prayed a desperate prayer for help." — Bob

Rita

In spite of all we do to stay close, sometimes things happen to one of us or in our relationship that can cause hurts. They may be the result of little things such as teasing and playfulness that went too far. Often they are the result of my thoughtlessness when Bob needs me to care. Whether conversations are light or serious, hurts can happen when I cut him off in mid-sentence. I send the message that what I have to say is more important than what he is saying. Hurts can also come from non-verbal cues which speak loudly and clearly about my interest in what Bob is saying. It is at these times that I need to ask for and grant forgiveness.

There is a difference between saying, "I'm sorry" and, "Will you forgive me, I forgive you." The word, "sorry" comes from the word sorrow. When I say "I'm sorry" it means that

I am trying to experience the sorrow that Bob is feeling. Today, it rolls off my lips without thinking. I sometimes wonder in the course of a day how many times I say those words without even thinking about it. I say it to a student I bump into in the hall, to a sales person if I drop something, when I don't hear what someone said, if I forget to do something I was supposed to do and inconvenience another, to name a few. In many cases, I say it to a stranger or someone with whom I have no relationship. In our marriage, I can say, "I'm sorry" without entering into the pain that Bob might be experiencing. While I still need to say these words, and I do, it is more important that I be mindful of asking for and granting forgiveness. That requires intimacy and trust and that I take ownership of my actions.

The following shows a time when Bob and I lived all of this in our relationship. By nature, I am a very sensitive person. Most of the time it is one of my best attributes, but at times it is my greatest detriment. Being sensitive helps me be aware of the needs of others, often before they even recognize them themselves. This helps me to be a responsive wife, mother, friend and teacher. On the other hand, at times I feel used and have to face the hurts that result from this sensitivity.

We were in a small prayer sharing group with a number of friends that we had come to know through our involvement in Marriage Encounter. We gathered monthly to pray together and share with one another how we were trying to live our marriages and receive help and support when needed. Outside our gatherings, we stayed in contact with each other and shared joys and sorrows. When a couple was facing a difficult time, one couple in the group would call all the others and ask for prayers - most of the time without indicating why prayers were needed. I did exactly that when one couple was facing difficult issues with one of their children. Since the couple had told a mutual friend who was in the group and he told us, I assumed it was okay to ask for prayers for them. The wife called with obvious anger in her voice and told me that I had no right to share their problems with anyone. I had not shared their problem; I didn't even know what it was until later. I had merely asked for prayers. I was surprised and taken back by her statement. Her anger with me did not go away and she spoke of it to others. When we tried on several occasions to resolve the issue with her and her husband, I acknowledged my responsibility and took ownership for any pain I caused her. I asked for forgiveness and when it wasn't granted greater hurts resulted. While she seemed to accept what I said, I interpreted what she said to mutual friends about the situation as a rejection of our friendship and everything I tried to do. When we were together I sensed a distance in our friendship. While it seemed to me that she was going along happily with our mutual friends she continued to reject any attempts I made to reconcile our friendship. We had been more than casual friends. We had shared some very intimate moments in our lives together and in the lives of our children. I have never been able to identify why this situation threw me the curve it did. As time passed, and the hurt intensified I sank into a deep depression. Since we had met them through our involvement in helping others, when I was depressed, I perceived the hurt to be the result of our being involved. I decided that I would never again put myself in a situation where I might experience this kind of rejection. In my mind, I judged that the pain of the rejection I felt was too great a price to pay to help others. I withdrew from nearly everyone and everything. I had a very negative attitude most of the time and didn't care about much of anything. Many days I found myself not even wanting to get dressed or do anything around the house that I didn't absolutely have to do. The world of daytime television and romance novels were my real companions. I felt hollow and empty inside and went through the motions in my relationship with Bob. Most days it was the hollow and empty feelings that actually comforted me. At least I felt something. Bob was very loving and even though we still wrote our letters and dialogued every day, I could never quite get Bob to understand what was happening to me when we tried to talk about it. My favorite quality about Bob is his optimism, so I found it difficult to see how he could relate to my feelings of despair. That just made the entire situation more difficult. To compound the situation, my greatest fear was that if he saw what I was going through as frivolous or rejected my feelings, I would be left with nothing. In my mind, feeling hollow and empty was better than feeling nothing at all. I went through the motions of being involved in some activities to which we were committed. Fr. Tom, a trusted priest friend, tried to help me/us work our way through the issue, but I couldn't get beyond my hurt. I remember telling him and Bob that I was never going to be involved in the lives of others again. We had done enough and this pain was proof that it required more than any human being should be asked to give. Bob's outrageous love for and commitment to me was relentless. In the beginning, my feelings didn't seem to have an effect on my relationship with him, but eventually doors began to close in aspects of our life together. It affected the fun that had always been so much a part of our lives. Everything was so serious. We both put on a good face when we went out so most people didn't see that somehow the spark had gone out of us. However, I knew it and felt trapped by that as well. This added to the intensity of the emptiness that I felt. We continued this way for over a year.

When we were married, I recognized that some sacrifices I would have to make in my life would require the help of God. If I didn't already believe in miracles, the resolution of this situation would make me a believer. Bob and I were asked, along with Fr. Tom, to present a couples' retreat in the neighboring diocese. Every part of me said, "No." I did not want to risk that this might result in another hurt. The two of them did not take my "no" for an answer, so I went through the motions in the preparation. Besides, I thought, we had been through enough weekends like this before that I could bluff my way through most of it. Whether I had a guardian angel or whether the Holy Spirit was active in my life I will never know. Maybe it's just the power of love that is the result of the commitment of God, Bob or a friend in my life. Somewhere in the course of working with the couples that weekend, I became aware of the rift that was occurring in our relationship and how my feelings were hurting Bob. As the retreat progressed, we decided to receive the Sacrament of Reconciliation together. It was something we had done many times before. During the Sacrament, we talked once again with Fr. Tom about the feelings I had and what was going on in our relationship. He suggested that before we went to bed that night we should re-exchange our wedding rings with a promise to each other that the three of us would continue to work through the problem after the weekend. Through the night and during the following morning, I wrestled with the idea that I was a sinner and that my sins were the cause of the problems between us. If things were to ever get better then I had to decide to try one more time to communicate how I felt to Bob and trust that he would accept my feelings. The burden of not sharing the feelings became greater than the feelings themselves as I wrote my reflection following the first presentation that morning. I was finally able to name for Bob the feelings I had and to describe them for him. I have no idea how long it took me to write. I remember finding it difficult to see what I was writing through the tears that streamed down my face as I asked him for forgiveness. When Bob read what I had written, he began to cry as well. He took me into his arms and held me until neither of us had any more tears to shed. Then we began to laugh. It felt so good to laugh again. I think we even jumped up and down on the bed like two little kids. There aren't words to adequately convey the feelings I felt but I was whole and once again felt complete inside rather than hollow and empty. Ironically enough, the next talk we were scheduled to give had as its focus how to heal hurts in a relationship. Needless to say, we had fresh material. I'm not sure if the couples actually understood what had happened, but they were acutely aware that powerful things happen when couples are willing to sacrifice themselves, identify hurts and ask for forgiveness. At the same time, I realized that all my relationships had been affected by my actions, so I asked Fr. Tom for forgiveness for any hurts I had caused him. When we got home, I gathered each of our children into my arms and asked them for forgiveness as well. We still see our friends occasionally, but our relationship with them is not the same. Maybe some day the grace of God will help the two of us heal our friendship. I have not given up hope, but neither do I spend as much time thinking about it the way I once did. What I can see today is that I sacrificed my pride, my fears and what I thought made me feel comfortable. Doing this changed my life forever.

Obviously, I am involved in the lives of other people. It has given me the courage to walk into my classroom every day and share my life story as I teach. The rewards have been unbelievable. I have been able to handle some subsequent life situations that were similar to this one without it having the same effect. In fact, I am a much stronger person today than I was before. I certainly live with the joy that comes when husbands and wives sacrifice for each other and I now know how the grace of God enables that to happen.

Bob

It only takes a moment to blurt out a response or use a word that I know will be hurtful to Rita, but it's out of my mouth before I can stop it. Sometimes I do something that hurts and then wonder, "What was I thinking?" Because my best efforts are never good enough, I have to be ready to express my sorrow to Rita over the hurt I have caused. Even more importantly, I have to ask her for forgiveness so that healing can take place.

I am a person who tends to look ahead and I don't take much time to look back at my life. When I retired from college teaching, I had many great memories of my years as a teacher, of my students and of my accomplishments. There were also some things that I wished I had done differently. But none of that was my focus. I told my colleagues at a retirement party that I wasn't retiring to stop work, but for the opportunity to do something different with the rest of my life.

Except for Rita and my children and grandchildren, I tend to approach relationships with people in a similar way. When I am working with people and trying to accomplish something with them, I go at it with a passion and that

includes my relationship with them. When it is time to go on
to other things, I keep my memories, but I find myself looking ahead to the next project I am about to tackle and the new
people I will meet.

When something goes wrong in a relationship I will do
my best to repair it, but when that fails, I decide that I can't
reconcile, so I put it behind me and move on. There is always
something ahead that will be more fruitful.

I was hurt in the incident with our friends that Rita described. After an initial period of anger and resentment, I
believed the relationship we had with this couple was pretty
much over. I thought the wife was incapable of understanding
the effect of her actions. It was hard to let it go, but I didn't
let it get to me and I tried to get on with my life. I didn't understand Rita's hurt or her inability to move on from it.

As time went on and Rita became withdrawn, she wanted us to withdraw from all of our volunteer commitments
and even our social life. I probably could have handled those
things, but she also withdrew from me. I couldn't figure out
how to connect with her. We had been through many years of
feeling close to each other and enjoying each other's company,
but during this time we lost the fun in our lives. As this situation persisted over weeks and then months, I became very
frightened. We were still going through the motions, trying
to communicate, praying together and making love, but I had
lost my best friend and I was afraid that I would never get
her back. I desperately wanted Rita to come out of it, but I
didn't know how to help. I was angry with her for not getting over it. During that time I found myself becoming very
short with her, and on a couple of occasions I snapped, at her.
I had never treated Rita that way and I instantly regretted
what I had said.

When we got the call asking us to give the retreat, Rita was sitting next to me saying, "No!" but I said, "Yes." I have no idea why. Since I had committed us to the weekend, we began to prepare for it. Rita's heart wasn't in it, but I kept pushing and hoping that I could get her to respond. When we arrived at the retreat on Friday evening, we were getting the conference room ready when we got into a disagreement over something I can't now recall. Here we were, trying to lead other couples into a better relationship and we couldn't get ourselves together. I didn't say anything to Rita then, but I decided that I would do anything I could to get us through this, and I prayed a desperate prayer for help. I told God that I would do whatever it took to get our relationship back, even though I had no idea what that would require.

Even talking with Fr. Tom didn't seem to help. He asked us to think about it overnight, but nothing was really resolved. The next morning, Rita's reflection was a love letter to me expressing her sorrow for the past months and asking me for forgiveness. I eagerly granted forgiveness and begged forgiveness for my failure to support her. We cried together and held each other for a long time.

This process began an important healing in our relationship. I was quite wary for a while afterward - hoping, but not knowing, what would happen the next time Rita was in a potentially hurtful situation. My fears were unfounded. The change in her was dramatic. She seemed to get better as each day went by. She is stronger now than ever before and I still marvel at how she can handle difficult situations with surprising ease.

When we each asked for and granted forgiveness to the other, we started a process of healing that has allowed us to get back the joy and playfulness that we cherish. There is a saying that whatever doesn't kill you will make you stronger. I believe that is what happened to us. Rita can still be upset about something that happens at work or in our families, but she is so strong that I have lost my fear that she will be hurt and withdraw from me again. That's awesome!

We could not resolve this situation without sacrifice. In some way, each of us had to make a decision to get us through it and each of us had to be willing to sacrifice and fight to undo the damage to our relationship. When I look back on it, that weekend looks to me like we were set up to get the healing going. God works in mysterious ways. In the end, I had to give up my desire to make Rita be like me and had to stop trying to control the situation while continuing to love her. I believe that my desperate prayer for help and my willingness to do whatever it took helped set the stage for the healing we found and our return to the relationship we cherished. The result was beyond my expectations.

Hints, Tips and Things We Learned Along the Way

* Find ways to make forgiveness, even of little things, part of your relationship on a regular basis. We have a practice of holding hands during the Lord's Prayer when we go to Mass together. When we get to the words, "Forgive us our trespasses..." we squeeze each other's hand as a sign that we are asking for forgiveness and granting forgiveness for anything we might have done recently to hurt the other. Even when everything is going well and we are close, it keeps us aware of our need to forgive and be forgiven. It makes seeking forgiveness easier when the hurt is larger and must be dealt with explicitly.

* A hurt cannot be healed until you recognize that it exists. Have the courage to face hurts. If one of you is hurt then it must be faced even if the other doesn't immediately see it. A major hurdle could arise when one of you feels hurt more than the other. Some individual situations just need to be forgiven and forgotten without major time spent on them. There has to be time for fun, joy and celebration in your lives.

* Forgiveness is crucial and it is a decision. Always forget how your spouse may have hurt you; **never** forget how you have hurt your

spouse. This is not meant to lay guilt on you but to be aware that you will hurt your spouse, sometimes deliberately and sometimes unwittingly.

❋   If the Sacrament of Reconciliation is part of your faith, consider making it a part of your healing process.

❋   Celebrate your relationship in some way when you have finished the process of forgiveness and healing. Sex may be a part of this, but never the only way to do so.

❋   Hurts may also come from outside your relationship but if the hurt is big enough it will eventually come between the two of you.

❋   Ultimately unresolved hurts will cause inappropriate behaviors toward each other.

❋   In some relationships hurts are that proverbial "800 pound gorilla" that lives in your house.

❋   In some relationships the hurts may cause a major explosion when least expected.

❋   Reflecting back on what we learned from this experience, Rita, and probably Bob, should have sought professional help. If you need it, get professional help.

Questions to Help Guide Your Discussion/ Dialogue

Remember to share your feelings along with your responses to these questions.

1. Where did I find me /us in Bob and Rita's story?

2. Have I hurt you today? More importantly do I know if I have?

3. What behaviors do I exhibit when I respond to hurts both in and out of our relationship?

4. Am I easily hurt and do I hold on to hurts?

5. What do I need to do to let go of hurts?

6. Are there areas in our relationship where we need to explore forgiveness and healing?

7. What makes it easy (difficult) for me to ask you to forgive me? (two questions)

8. What makes it easy (difficult) for me to forgive you? (two questions)

9. What is the "800 pound gorilla" in our relationship?

10. Recall a time when you forgave each other. How did this affect your relationship?

FACING THE CHALLENGES OF MONEY

"head me off at the pass" — Bob

"…using his money." — Rita

Bob

When I was growing up on the farm, we always had plenty of good food to eat. We raised beef, pork and chicken and my mother always had a large garden. She canned or froze summer fruits and vegetables for the winter. My dad used to joke that the farmer's motto was, "Eat the best and sell the rest."

In other areas, money was always limited. My mother sewed dresses for my sisters to save money. We never received an allowance and I usually had very little cash to spend. In the summers from sixth grade on, I worked for a local truck farmer when I could be spared on our farm. I picked green beans and tomatoes and one summer spent weeks on a tractor cultivating long rows of tomatoes. The work gave me a little spending money, but I put most of it away to pay for college.

I was fortunate to have a full scholarship to college. It paid all my expenses, with a little spending money left over, but money was still tight. I can remember taking more than an hour to decide whether I could afford to spend four dollars on a transistor radio.

I learned from my father to always look for the best deal. I tend to take my time checking out any major purchase to be sure that the deal is right. Car salesmen wish they had never met me. Rita gets impatient with the amount of time I take and never knows when I will decide that the time is right to proceed with the purchase. In fact, I don't know until I'm there.

I keep careful records of our finances. Computers have made record-keeping easier and I always have a mental approximation of the status of our accounts. I check the credit card balances online at least once a week.

Just before our wedding, as we were trying to merge what little finances we had, I looked at Rita's checkbook, saw what looked to me like a mess, and decided that I would take care of our money. That probably wasn't fair, but she didn't seem to mind and that was the way it has been ever since.

In the early years of our marriage, I made most of the day-to-day financial decisions. If there wasn't enough money to pay all the bills in full, I would decide which bills to pay and which to hold back or pay partially. I might tell Rita what I had done, but it was information, not consultation.

On larger purchases, we had an unwritten agreement that we would make the decision together. Mostly Rita went along with what I wanted to do, but occasionally she would object. In those situations there was little discussion - she would just say no and I would usually let the subject drop.

We always tended to have different priorities about spending money. I like to spend it on cars, tools and electronics. While I like to be dressed well, I don't have much enthusiasm for spending money on clothing. Rita likes to spend money on clothes for her and for me and on items for the house and kids. Early on I learned to "test the waters" by mentioning an item that I would like to buy to see what reaction it would get. Rita learned to "head me off at the pass" and squelch such items. Sometimes I would get a response like, "We don't need that!", even though I was just commenting on an interesting piece of electronics I saw advertised.

We got along reasonably well in this way for years. There was some tension over money, but we didn't fight about it. We had our signals worked out and managed to keep our finances in good order, but we never openly discussed our thoughts and feelings about money.

When we finally started to discuss finances openly, I was surprised to discover that Rita saw our money as my money and that she was just allowed to spend some of it. That was never my attitude or intent. This alerted me to try to involve Rita more in the financial process. I realized that I needed to give her more information and an opportunity for input, even though I was handling the mechanics of paying the bills.

A couple of times we tried a formal budgeting process but it never seemed to work for us. We have learned to budget and set priorities in an informal way. We have frequent discussions about how we want to spend money in the short and longer terms. If we need to work with some figures, I usually do that and report back to Rita. For a guy who likes to have everything worked out, it seems odd that we should do it this way, but it works for us. It helps that we are both willing to delay purchases or abandon them entirely when they don't fit our financial plans. A few years ago, when the lease was up on a very nice car, replacing it with a similar vehicle would have stretched our finances, so I drove a less expensive car for the next lease term.

While we still like to spend money in different ways, the discussions we have had and the knowledge each of us now has about how the other approaches money has served to reduce the tension associated with the subject. As we are approaching retirement, we are keeping each of us fully involved in our financial planning. We are organizing papers and reviewing such things as our wills and insurance plans. We hope to go into retirement with a solid plan and also to be prepared if one of us would have to go into retirement alone.

For several years we heard other couples talk about tithing, giving a percentage of income, to charity. Some were quite enthusiastic about it and made claims about God rewarding them with even more money. I was always skeptical about that sort of claim, but I did think that we were very blessed and should be giving more to charity. When we attended a talk on tithing, we were encouraged to give a percentage of our income to the parish and an equal percentage to other charities. The speaker convinced us that we could have the extra money for charity if we would set it aside in advance - we would no longer look on that portion of our income as ours, but as the amount we were giving back to God in thanksgiving for our blessings. With some misgivings about what seemed to be a large amount of money and concern about being able to pay our bills, we decided to give it a try.

With the money set aside, there was no longer a question of whether we had money to give; it was just a matter of deciding on the recipients. We were able to increase our contributions to the Church and pick out a couple of worthy causes to receive regular contributions. We were pleasantly surprised to find that the extra amount we were giving never once kept us from paying our bills.

Tithing has changed my attitude toward money. It helps me to remember that our money is a gift from God and gives me the satisfaction of knowing that we are showing our gratitude. I see the rest of our money as a gift that we can enjoy and use for good for ourselves and others. I am a worrier when it comes to money, but tithing and becoming more conscious that God takes care of us has helped me to relax about it.

Rita

The area in our relationship that has created the most tension is finances. It hasn't mattered whether we were on a very limited budget or today when we are reasonable financially secure. Money is the area that Bob worries about the most.

After my father died, my family was not as financially secure as we had been. We didn't go without essentials and we had some luxuries, but from the time I reached adolescence, I was taking care of a lot of my basic financial needs. I babysat for neighbors and nieces and nephews. The money I made went for a few luxuries, but mostly I used it to furnish my wardrobe. I didn't have an actual job until after I graduated from high school and then part time and summer jobs through college. The money I earned went for tuition and all my personal college expenses. There was never a lot, but I managed to have all the things I needed. If I purchased something I wanted or needed then I did without something else. In general, I knew what my finances were and my concern was the bigger picture, not the minute details. In the end it all worked out for me.

When we were first married, I taught while Bob was a full time graduate student with a fellowship. We used to joke about the fact that even with the little money (a combined income of $7000), we had more money than either of us had before. From the beginning Bob pretty much took care of paying bills; partly because he had more time, but dealing with numbers and understanding all about them is also a talent of his. We did talk generally about how much we had and how we were going to spend it. Neither of us spent very much money at one time without consulting the other.

As time passed and I stopped working outside our home, I developed the attitude that the money we had was Bob's, not ours, even though we referred to it as ours. I was privileged to spend some of it, especially if it was for food and necessary items. I found it easier to spend money on the kids but difficult to spend on myself or to buy gifts for Bob. It seemed strange to buy a gift for him using his money. I'm not sure where the attitude came from, but even though I now work full time, I still hesitate at times about spending money on myself.

As we explored this area, I was able to tell Bob about a comment he frequently made when I returned from shopping. Even if he seemed excited about what I purchased, he might ask, "How much did you spend?" Immediately, I judged myself as not quite measuring up to his expectations. It seemed to me that I was a little girl who wasn't quite capable of making right decisions, especially if I had spent money on myself.

Eventually I told him about this. We shared our feelings and discussed it. I learned that he wasn't checking up on me. He was trying to keep a running total in his head of the amount in the checkbook or on the credit card statement. The discussion made him aware of how he got the information. Today, he can easily get it online. Now I tell him up front what I've spent while we're talking about the purchases and I give him the receipts. I am freer to voice my feelings, ask if there is a problem with our finances, or ask if he would like to spend the money on something else. That then leads to other discussions.

Through the years we have attended workshops that helped us to look at our attitudes about the way we spend money and the priorities we needed to set to use the funds we have. We've had various insurance and financial planners interview us and try to help us set goals. We never quite fit with the options they gave us and many times I found myself filling out their survey because it was something I had to do as part of the process. Whether or not we would ever own a boat or vacation home or whether I have a fur coat was not very interesting to me. The values we wanted to live were more important. We did set some priorities. While my joke today is to drive the Winnebago to the Hilton on vacation, we did camp in a tent with our children when they were young. It gave us vacations we could afford and our children saw many parts of the country they might otherwise not have seen. In our planning, we decided that we would take a major family vacation the summer after each of our children's junior year of high school. It was their official last family vacation. After that they were expected to work to help pay college expenses. We did various things with them including Disney World, Washington, D.C., and Tampa, Florida. Our youngest even managed to go to Hawaii with us because we had frequent flyer miles from paying college tuition.

In the process of setting priorities, it became important for us to have our children attend both Catholic high schools and colleges. Fortunately, our children received scholarships and financial aid but it was our decision to provide private educations for them. We had to make some other sacrifices. Early on we decided that I would not return to working outside our home until our oldest went to college. Then my salary would go toward paying tuition rather than being part of our general income. This allowed me to stay home with our children until our youngest was in first grade. When I returned to teaching, we managed to juggle our schedules for one of us to be home when he was.

While our list of things to acquire didn't always fit those of a financial planner, we had individual and joint things that we wanted to purchase at some future date. At times we got to the point of having enough money to purchase something and found that we didn't want it any more. Dining room furniture was on my list for 25 years. It was near the bottom of the list most of that time. Vacations and educations always seemed to have a higher priority. It became a running joke with us. I would set an arbitrary date by which we would buy it. Some family event or significant wedding anniversary headed my list of appropriate times. The empty dining room in two houses provided a play area for the kids when they were young and space for a computer room as they grew older. Finally, we had a lull in paying college tuition and my goal was to have the furniture before our daughter got married. We bought the furniture, and a few months later she announced her engagement. I like having long family meals around the table, especially as our family has expanded to include spouses and grandchildren.

While other areas of our relationship are playful, money talks usually are not. We may be dreaming, but the discussions are serious. Recognizing this has helped me to relax more.

Hints, Tips and Things We Learned Along the Way

* While one person may be better at paying the bills and keeping records, both spouses need to be included when setting priorities and in financial planning.

* Formal budgets work very well for some people. While we have never been very successful at making and keeping a formal budget, one of our sons and his wife keep a very detailed budget and follow it closely. For them it works very well.

* Save some money. Emergencies arise and eventually we all hope to retire. Having some money on hand can make both situations easier.

* Learn to distinguish between needs and wants. Needs require priority, wants can be deferred. Some couples find this very difficult when providing financially for their children.

* Money can become a control issue in a relationship. The controller may be the person who handles the mechanics or the one who shows no interest and accepts no responsibility.

* Give some money away. You need to try this to experience its value. Have a discussion and pick an amount that you will give to others each month or each year.

* Managing finances will always be part of your relationship. Don't try to solve all the issues in a short period of time. The discussions in this area need to be handled on a regular basis. Most of the discussions need to be done multiple times as situations present themselves.

* It can't be serious all the time. It is okay to occasionally spend money frivolously and not worry about it.

* Learn to laugh about failures along the way.

* If you need professional help in this area, seek it out.

Questions to Help Guide Your Discussion/ Dialogue

Remember to share your feeling as you respond to the questions.

1. Where did I find me/us in Bob and Rita's story?

2. A series of questions to use over a period of time:

    a. What do I like most about the way I manage money?

    b. What do I like least about the way I manage money?

    c. What do I like most about the way you manage money?

    d. What do I like least about the way you manage money?

    e. What do I think we need to do individually and as a couple to better manage our finances?

3. Another set of questions to use over a period of time:

    a. What did I learn from my mother about managing money?

    b. What did I learn from my father about managing money?

    c. How do I see my responses to the above affecting how I handle money?

4. Do we work together to set financial priorities? Do we need to improve? How?

5. Am I comfortable with the charitable contributions we make?

6. Do we ever spend money to enhance our marriage?

7. How does providing for our children's wants rather than needs affect the way we manage our money?

8. If we could spend some money (amount depending on financial circumstances), what would I like to do?

Seeking a Balance: Jobs/ Careers and Relationship

"…wanted me to be successful…" — Bob

"…more important than the money." — Rita

Bob

My job has been an important part of my life. It has offered me financial reward as well as a sense of self-worth and affirmation in the things I have done.

I was fairly young when I realized that farming was not the life for me. Many members of my extended family hoped that I would become a priest, but by eighth grade I knew that I would not. I was always interested in many things, especially science and mathematics. By the time I graduated from high school, I had decided to become an electrical engineer. In the summer between my first and second years of college, I worked in the engineering test labs of a large corporation where I saw first-hand the work that engineers were doing.

I found that the work didn't exactly suit me, so I switched to physics as my major. I liked applying the theory to problems and I was fascinated by the ability of my professors to get right to the heart of an issue.

By the middle of my junior year, it was clear that I could make it as physics major, but that I couldn't compete well with the other students who would go on to get doctorates. At the suggestion of one of my professors, I started to take some courses in the field of education. I went on to get a masters in education and then into a doctoral program in science education. I completed most of the program, but never finished. I thought that I could do some good by engaging in educational research, but events in my life put me into a classroom where I could see directly the rewards for my efforts. That is where I stayed.

I never really had to look for a job. The university gave me a lead on a one-year job in a high school, and then a friend alerted me to a permanent job teaching mathematics and physics in a community college. I quickly got involved on college committees and with the faculty in campus politics. I received considerable support and affirmation from my faculty colleagues. With a job and two children, I found it difficult to work on my dissertation and when I did, it wasn't going well. Eventually I dropped out of the doctoral program.

I continued teaching in the community college for thirty years. There was satisfaction in working with students. As electronic calculators replaced slide rules and computers replaced much of the laboratory equipment that had been in use for half a century or more, I enjoyed introducing new technology in my classroom and laboratory. I had the privilege of working on committees that affected the lives of students and college employees. I take satisfaction in looking at the history of an institution that was only a couple of years old when I joined it and knowing that I had a part in creating some significant pieces of that history.

One of the advantages of my job was its security. I knew many people who lost jobs and went through difficult periods of unemployment until they found other jobs. I never had to go through that. The job also provided a flexibility that most jobs cannot. Although I often worked many hours every week, I had to be on campus for my classes and office hours, but I could prepare lessons and tests or grade papers anytime and anywhere I liked. This made it possible for me to do our Christmas shopping on weekday mornings and grade papers on the weekend. It gave me the option at times of going to our children's school events during the workday.

Perhaps the most important benefit of teaching was the intellectual stimulation it provided. I thrive on having several things going on in my life at once. There was always something new to try in the classroom. I taught more than one class at a time and the campus committees often involved subjects that were far from my teaching field. As the chairperson of a committee dealing with employee health insurance, I learned a great deal about the health insurance industry and how trends in the industry affected the college health insurance program. I enjoyed going to professional meetings to learn new teaching techniques and frequently shared my experiences with others. When this wasn't enough, I got involved in consulting work in a variety of fields. This work was usually challenging and I enjoyed helping a business to solve its problems. At times consulting also provided some significant extra income for the family.

For the most part, my teaching career was good for us. The flexibility it allowed made it possible for us to have more time together than many married couples. The downside was that it offered infinite possibilities to do more and more. When I would get an idea for a better way to present a topic in one of my classes, I could spend many hours working out the lab techniques or creating new materials. When I came up with a new written assignment, I could suddenly add hours of paper grading to my schedule. These were the things that had me retreating to the den after dinner most nights to be prepared for the next day or week of classes.

We had many discussions about my job and its demands on my time. In later years, I reduced my involvement some-what and turned down some committee work. We tried to maintain some balance between my career and the needs of our marriage. Most of the time I think the balance was a little off in one direction or another, but usually not too far. Sometimes grading papers kept me from spending time with Rita. Other times, spending time with Rita made students wait longer to have their graded papers returned. It was never a big issue for us, but there were times when Rita complained that I was spending too much time on my work.

After thirty years, I was offered a great opportunity to retire. It provided a good income and some additional incen-tives. While I still liked teaching, this opened the possibility to do something else with a part of my life. It was a treat to spend the first year at home living at a reduced pace and catching up on some things I had wanted to do for a long time. When that started to lose its allure, I found some consulting work for a while, and then went back to teaching at the col-lege part-time. With Rita working full-time, I found that I needed the stimulation of teaching and the contact with people.

A few years ago, the high school where Rita teaches, had an opening for a religion teacher and a very limited number of applicants. For many years, Rita had shared the things she did in her job, and on a couple of occasions, I had even helped her with high school retreats. I had great admiration for her work and found the idea of teaching religion attractive. It was a big change in subject matter for me, but I had some college theology and had written a column on religious subjects for many years. After giving it some thought and prayer, I told Rita that I was thinking about applying. She was surprised. I think her first words were, "What? Are you nuts?!" After some long discussions about it and with her approval, I applied for and got the job, with Rita as my department chair.

My first year was extremely busy, but it went well. The year was made easier by the constant support and assistance I received from my department chair. She wanted me to be successful as much as I did. It was interesting to be a new teacher again in many ways, but a very experienced teacher in others. We rode to work together which gave us lots of time to talk about us as well as our jobs. In the following years, I was able to contribute more to curriculum development and other department concerns, in addition to doing a better job of teaching.

Having Rita stay at home with the children when they were small had advantages for me. She was able to take care of much of the business of running the family during the day and that gave us more time in the evenings and weekends to be together and to have involvements like Marriage Encounter or our parish organizations. When the job opportunity arose and Rita decided to go back to work, we discussed the pros and cons at length. I was in favor of giving it a try, even though I knew that I would have to pick up more work at home. When Rita became discouraged in her new job and talked about quitting, I encouraged her to hang in there a little longer and tried to give her all the moral support I could. The situation improved and I am pleased that she has found teaching so rewarding. I see her as the master teacher and the one I would like to be like when I grow up.

The income from Rita's work was a tremendous boost to our finances and allowed us to keep our children in Catholic schools. Since then it has supplemented my pension and has allowed us to do some of the things we've dreamed about, especially travel. We continue to discuss retirement and assume the time is drawing nearer. While I have stopped teaching at the high school, Rita continues. I still need to be busy and have multiple activities. I believe that we will each know when the time is right to fully retire. Until then we will continue to make decisions together about our future.

Rita

From the time I was in third or fourth grade, I remember wanting to be a teacher. I was a very good student and while no one in my immediate family had ever gone to college, I wanted to go. I continued to think about going to college even when others told me it was not financially feasible or just a waste of time because I would eventually get married, have children and not use the education I had acquired. Not many students in my high school class went to college. During my senior year, with the encouragement of a few teachers, I applied to several colleges and was accepted. With scholarships, loans and part time jobs, I graduated four years later with a degree in history, a teaching certificate to teach social studies in junior high and high school, and enough credits to teach religion.

I get great satisfaction in learning and helping others to learn. The fascination with learning continues today. It is perhaps one of the reasons I don't see retirement as enticing yet.

As some members of my family predicted, I did get married the summer I graduated from college. I applied for a teaching position in Chicago so that Bob could go to graduate school. Applying was part of the fun and adventure of planning our life together. I was offered and accepted a teaching position in a north suburban Chicago Catholic high school. I taught history and religion for three years and until we had a baby. I didn't consider my going back to work after he was born. As the years passed and we had more children, I missed getting out of the house and having contact with people, but I used my teaching skills to help our children excel in school. The volunteer activities, especially when we were in leadership roles, provided an intellectual challenge. I used many of my talents and grew as a person, and even better we were doing it together. In the back of my head, I always thought that I would eventually have a career outside our home but I wasn't sure what it would be. I just didn't know when or what I would do. When our youngest was three and our oldest was approaching college age, I began to look for some career possibilities. We were facing college expenses and I knew I wanted to do more than volunteer. I began to look for something that I could do where I would be rewarded financially. I took steps to renew my teaching certificate and even considered a total career change by taking an introductory course in being a travel agent. At this time, a neighbor and a friend offered to care for our youngest if, on occasion, I wanted to substitute at the Catholic high schools where our older two children were enrolled.

At our daughter's school I met a woman who taught religion. During free periods and lunch breaks when I subbed, we shared many conversations about values we both held and what we wanted in our lives. A few years later, she was at another Catholic high school and our youngest was in first grade, when she recommended me for a full time religion position. I was to teach for a quarter but I stayed to finish the year and that began the career path that I am still on today. Along the way I worked as a campus minister, began a retreat program, became a department chair, and served on numerous committees. Since I changed schools, I am a classroom teacher, chair the religion department, and am involved in student led retreats. Teaching religion to teenagers, while incredibly challenging, has brought more rewards than other jobs I had considered. While I worried about retirement income, I accepted that teaching in a Catholic high school was not going to make me wealthy. We have talked about this frequently and agreed that what I am doing is more important than the money. Somehow we have had enough to do the things we want to do. I am learning to trust that I will be okay as I age.

Throughout the years since I resumed my teaching career, I have thought about pursuing a master's degree and have been encouraged by various administrators to do so. On occasion I have taken graduate courses and periodically gather information on degree programs. In many ways, I approach getting a master's degree in the same way I did getting dining room furniture. While I would like to say that I have one, as it would get me a small salary increase and would provide an intellectual challenge, there are always more things I would like to do with the time and money. One of the reasons I began to teach again was to help pay for our children's college educations. With that cost, there was not enough money for me to pursue a degree as well. I believe that the other things I have done with my life have given me experiences that are as helpful to my students as an official degree. Even now as we are finished with tuitions, there are other things like travel that still are higher on my priority list and enrich my teaching. Perhaps I will get a master's degree some day. The idea remains on the list of things I would like to do before I die.

We still struggle with how to juggle careers and marriage. It is a contributing factor to the reason I have not pursued a master's program. My career is temporary, while our marriage is forever. I know that at this point in my life having a career enhances our relationship. I struggle with the time commitment and physical energy required to teach the way I do. When he retired, Bob's schedule allowed him to pick up some of the things I once did. He picked up more of the day to day household chores. It gave us more time together, especially on weekends. When Bob accepted the high school job, we decided to pay others to do some jobs for us. This lets us do the things we want and need to do, visit our children and grandchildren, have social time with friends and be involved in volunteer activities. Each year I reevaluate the role my teaching has on our marriage.

There have been some difficult times with parents, students and members of my department. On more than one occasion I have seriously considered quitting, but when I weigh all the pros and cons and with Bob's encouragement, teaching adolescents is the right thing for me and for us at the moment. In the not too distant future I will look for something else to do with my life that doesn't require the time and energy commitment that teaching does. Maybe that's when I will get that master's degree. In the meantime, my job continues to be a source of positive growth for me. Students constantly affirm what I do for them in their lives and alumni drop by as well. Many adults in the school seek me out for advice. Being a department chair is an intellectual challenge and a source of great satisfaction as I develop curriculum and work with the teachers in the department. When Bob joined the faculty of the school in my department, a new challenge was added. I was, in a way, his "boss." It was an interesting and good challenge. While it created additional stress at the beginning of the first year, in the end we had three great years together. I no longer had to drive to school, we had wonderful discussions along the way and both grew as persons and teachers as we discussed the curriculum for the courses we taught. The most difficult part of it all was trying not to discuss school 24/7. While we tried to set aside non-school time, it had a way of taking whatever time we allowed.

Other than my first one, I never looked for a job or to change the one I had. Teaching at the school from which all of our children have graduated has had an extra bonus. We had great times together on the drive and I got to be part of their high school years in a way most parents never are.

When Bob taught at the college level I liked the flexible hours. He usually had breakfast with the kids, was home early afternoons and helped chauffeur them to activities. A school schedule allowed days off with the kids and holiday time together. Even when he taught summer school, the reduced schedule gave us weekend time for vacation, to go camping with the kids or visit grandparents. His schedule made it possible for us to do retreat weekends and have considerable time with our children.

Bob likes to have more than one thing going on at a time. After he taught for a while, he added consulting work to his schedule. I was concerned about the time commitment, but it seemed important to him and it was a way to supplement our income. While at times he was busier than I would have liked, consulting had deadlines and projects that were completed; this allowed us discussion time before he took on another project. There were times when I wished I could find something to do myself and we talked about that possibility. We considered starting a business together, but the right one never seemed to fall into place. Bob managed to keep just enough projects to make him and us happy with a lifestyle we enjoyed.

Hints, Tips and Things We Learned Along the Way

* Unless you are independently wealthy, you likely need some means of supporting yourself and your family. Jobs/careers do more than provide financial support; they help define who you are. The key is to find a balance between the demands of work, personal fulfillment, providing for the family and your commitment to each other.

* Recognize the self worth, the sense of purpose and fulfillment that comes from your job. If your job does not enhance your self-worth or personal fulfillment, consider the effect of this on your marriage. Talk about it frequently.

* While one parent may stay at home with the children, raising them is a two parent responsibility. To avoid stress and arguments, each parent's role needs to be discussed. Household tasks will need to be shared.

* Any job can be very demanding some of the time, but a job that is all-consuming most or all of the time cannot be good for a marriage. We know people who have changed jobs, not taken a job or turned down promotions to keep their marriage first.

* Wants and needs both enter into the choices you make about jobs. It helps to make better career decisions if you understand your needs and wants and the difference between the two.

* In any discussion of jobs and careers, be aware of both your present and future financial needs. When our kids were growing up, we tried to maintain a balance among family time and lifestyle, planning for their college educations and our retirement.

* Overemphasis on jobs at the expense of your relationship will likely create tension at various times. It helps to recognize that tension and to revisit priorities when it happens.

* Trade time for money or money for time. During the first half of our marriage, we lived on one income and did many jobs ourselves to save money. Now that we are both working, we hire professionals to do work around our house. This allows us to spend time with each other and our family.

Questions to Help Guide Your Discussion/ Dialogue

Remember to share your feelings along with your thoughts.

1. Where did I find me/us in Bob and Rita's story?

2. What do I like best/least about my job? (Two separate questions)

3. What do I like best/least about your job? (Two separate questions)

4. What/how does my job contribute to my sense of self-worth or personal fulfillment?

5. What effect does my/your job have on our relationship?

6. What would I be willing to sacrifice in my career to enhance my relationship with you?

7. What small, immediate changes could I make to give us more time together?

8. Do I recognize the difference between wants and needs and their effect on career choices we make?

9. What do we need to reevaluate to bring a better focus between our jobs and our relationship?

10. Have we found a balance between living in the present and planning for the future?

11. What do we need to change to bring a better balance between the present and the future?

CREATING SEXUAL INTIMACY

"...close the closet door..." — Bob

"...doesn't talk...just does 'it'..." — Rita

Bob

My formal preparation for sex in marriage consisted of a marriage preparation course I took in college and a brief session with the pastor of Rita's parish two days before our wedding. Since the pastor was embarrassed to mention the word, I have to discount that session. The college course did have value for me. I learned that sex has a purpose in keeping a couple close, as well as in creating babies. I remember the priest who taught the course talking about the importance that both partners be satisfied. I went into our marriage committed to caring for Rita's needs during sex.

At least from the first time I kissed Rita, I found her physically desirable. During our dating years, we did lots of hugging and kissing. One of the reasons I often got home so late from our dates is that I wanted so much to be with Rita and I didn't want to give up holding her close. Through our dating years, we discussed sex and speculated about what it would be like. It would have been so easy to go beyond hugging and kissing, but we were determined to wait.

On our wedding night, Rita wore a sexy white negligee and looked absolutely beautiful in it. Nevertheless, I took it off of her as quickly as I could. I didn't know how shy she might be, so I was very careful to be gentle and to ask before doing anything. I had never been naked in front of any woman and had never seen an adult woman naked. I bought a new pair of pajamas for our honeymoon, but I took them off that night and I don't think I ever put them back on. Somehow, being naked with Rita seemed natural. Part of the fun of our first days together was the process of becoming familiar with each other's bodies and learning how to physically love each other. I had read enough to think I knew how it was supposed to work, but sometimes we found it all rather awkward. Anyway, passion took over and it didn't really matter what I thought I knew and the awkward moments added to the fun.

Waiting to have sex made being married different from and so much better than not being married. It added a new dimension to our friendship. Our college marriage prep courses had given us material to discuss about sex, theoretically, before we were married. Those discussions allowed me to be relaxed with Rita and enjoy the process of learning the physical "how to." It wasn't necessary to be experienced or a "good" sex partner. Since we were both learning, being "good" simply meant talking to her and laughing at our awkwardness until we figured it out. Along the way we learned to talk to each other during sex and learned something about each other's likes and dislikes. As I told a friend who got married two weeks after we did, the good thing about being married to a teacher is that she keeps making you do it over until you get it right.

After a few years of marriage and as children arrived, our sexual activity never suffered from quality, but we struggled with quantity. After each child was born, the demands of a new baby affected everything in our lives, but especially the frequency of our physical love making. To compensate, I tended to get more involved in my job.

It was always clear to me that sex was good for us. When we became distant or disconnected, making love would bring me closer to Rita. It helped me to get rid of some of the tension from my job. Sometimes it was just fun and brought back the playfulness in our lives. I didn't know how it worked, but it helped me to get through the busy times and the stress that I sometimes felt. When we started to actively discuss our sexual relationship, I shared with Rita my feelings about my body and hers. I told her how I felt about her role in our sexual relationship and about my own. I listened to everything she had to say about her feelings and thoughts in these areas. I reflected on the ways that I wanted to be loved and listened as Rita shared her wants and needs with me.

These dialogues allowed us to grow in many ways. I wasn't so good at expressing my need for sex. Rita never said no to me when I asked, but I didn't like to take the risk that she might, so I didn't ask very often. Sometimes I knew that she was tired and I didn't want to pressure her. I learned to ask by hinting, mostly in non-verbal ways, like giving her an extra long kiss or an extra hug or a squeeze in the right place. This allowed her to say "yes" by responding to my hints or "no" by just ignoring them. It was easier that way. I couldn't tell much about Rita's desire for sex. She hardly ever asked. Maybe I was hinting often enough that she could simply decide to respond when she was ready.

At a friend's suggestion, we decided that, for a month, we would have a discussion each day about whether we were going to have sex. One of us would ask the other, "Are we going to have sex today?" to start the discussion. As the month progressed, we found that we could be more up front about the whole subject. Rita could ask me questions like, "How important is it to you?" or "Can you wait until morning?" I could say to her, "I know you have had an exhausting day. Are you too tired for sex this evening?" The open discussion and our honesty with each other took away the disappointment I often felt when Rita didn't respond to my hints. When one of us said "no" to the other, it came with a reason and often a commitment to some activity in the near future. (No, we didn't have sex every day that month.)

Many people have told us that they don't like to talk about sex because they want it to be spontaneous. Sometimes it is. One Sunday in the summer we had returned from Mass and went upstairs to change clothes. We were both in our walk-in closet and I grabbed Rita to give her a kiss. Before long we became very passionate. The problem was that our children were elsewhere in the house as were some neighborhood children. We decided that we could lock our bedroom door and close the closet door and avoid detection. We had a great time! We have told this story to couples in workshops, referring to it as "Closet Sex." A year or so after one of these workshops, a couple who had attended came up to us and proudly showed us their "Closet Sex" baby.

Most of the time, spontaneity is a myth. If we actually depended on an unplanned moment to have sex, there would be much less sexual activity in our marriage. There were many times when we pretended that the sex just happened, but that was just a little game we played. Most of the time at least one of us had been making plans in the hope that sexual activity would result. I would come home from work and spend a little extra time kissing Rita or sneak up behind her and kiss her on the neck. The signals were there, but later, at bedtime, we pretended that it was spontaneous because we hadn't spoken about it.

Getting rid of the myth of spontaneity had a number of advantages. We could look ahead a few hours or a couple of days and agree that we had a date. It helped us to have sex more often because it had a place in the schedule. Spontaneous sex is great when it happens, but planning opens up other possibilities. We can decide to meet somewhere other than our bedroom or we can gather together candles and massage oils. Knowing that sex is on the schedule makes it possible to prepare for it by romancing each other ahead of time. It leads to extra hugs, kisses and special squeezes during the day. If I'm out, I may pick up some flowers for Rita. We have sometimes planned a special meal designed to lead to sex. There is also something to be said for having time to think about it and anticipate the fun ahead, although it has messed with my efficiency on a work day.

While this exercise of asking lasted officially for a month, its effects have lasted for years. I am more willing to ask Rita for sex. I find it easier to wait when she says, "It's been a long day - can you wait until tomorrow evening?" That removes the element of rejection and I can anticipate the future. She willingly loves me if I say that I can't wait, but I am usually willing to wait.

I wasn't explicitly aware of it, at first, but I think our experience of sex from the beginning was that it has different purposes at different times. There were times when we were focused on getting pregnant and our activities were oriented toward Rita's cycle. But those times were rare in all of our years of marriage. Much of the time there was a possibility of pregnancy, but the activity was more immediately aimed at enjoying each other. Children are no longer a possibility, but sexual intercourse continues to offer us many benefits. Sex can help us to heal hurts and it can be a celebration of our relationship. It can be very passionate or somewhat quiet. Sometimes one of us is raring to go while the other isn't very interested. I have found that there is much to be gained by letting sex be what it is at this moment. I think of sex like eating – sometimes I like steak and all the trimmings, but that would become boring if I had it every day. It's nice to have a salad or a hamburger once in a while. Sometimes the big production with lots of time and caresses and all the fun that goes with those things is just what we need. At other times, we're both content to just be together and have the satisfaction of loving each other before rolling over and going to sleep. It isn't always necessary for both of us to reach orgasm. One of Rita's great gifts to me is a "quickie" when time is short or she doesn't feel a great need. Even in these situations, our activity brings us closer to each other. Since we have adopted the attitude that today our sexual activity is what it is, I have rarely been disappointed with the outcome.

We look for a variety of ways to keep sex fun and interesting. We might both read a chapter of a book on sex and then share our feelings about trying a different position or action suggested. Some of the things we tried and enjoyed; others we decided were not for us. It has been freeing for me to be able to bring up a sexual topic for discussion and know that I am free to speak my mind and trust that Rita will do the same without expecting that an action must follow.

As our children were growing up, we tried to get away from home occasionally to have time just for us. We told people that we were looking for warmer weather, a place where we could take walks on the beach or we wanted to see the sunset from Waikiki. In reality, we also wanted to get away for the sex. It is good for us to be away from our family, from familiar surroundings, our jobs and chores and the normal responsibilities of life, so that I can concentrate just on us. New locations and new activities help to keep sex fresh and exciting. They increase my desire and bring back memories of the awkwardness and fun of being newlyweds.

Rita

I have no doubt that it was the right thing for us to wait to have sex. I tell my students that it is the best wedding gift I received and it hasn't worn out yet. It is the one thing that Bob and I have only done with the other. Like everything else in our marriage, this has been a journey. There have been occasional detours and a few potholes along the way, but a wonderful journey. For someone who grew up believing that a good Catholic girl doesn't talk about sex, she just does "it", I've come a long way. I remember how vulnerable I felt the morning after our wedding when the negligee had been tossed aside and Bob asked if it was okay if he looked at my naked body in the light; to finding myself in the shower with him a few days later; to having sex outdoors; to giving sexuality workshops for couples; to sharing with my students; and even more so, to put it in black and white in this book which our children may read.

Along the way we have had many discussions with friends and family, attended and given workshops and convention speeches. Doing that has helped me develop the ease and openness that I have today. I can talk about sex with and in front of our children and I don't find it difficult to discuss sex and sexuality with my students. Occasionally I can still be embarrassed and turn bright red even in front of my students when something doesn't come out the way I intended, but I have come to accept my body, my sexuality and the role that sex has in keeping me close to Bob.

I talked about sex with Bob before we were married; especially what I had learned in the marriage course I took. After all the talking we did, I knew nothing about the reality of physical love. The talking helped us to create an atmosphere later in which I could talk about my wants and needs and likes and dislikes. We talked about what we did and new things to try. It led us to experiment with new ideas, like taking a shower together and having sex there or leaving the dishes on the table and ending up on the floor halfway to our bedroom. As time has passed, I do find it easier to voice all the things that are running through my head and to not assume that Bob knows what I want and like.

Understanding that, in addition to creating a baby, making physical love to each other helps to create a special bond, was also important. Knowing that, I could indeed have fun exploring various places to have sex even in our own house— we haven't quite made it to the dining room table where friends have or to the lush green grass on a golf course in Mexico only to have the sprinklers go off. We have found our walk in closet and the squeaky bed in the room above Bob's parent's bedroom. The possibilities are endless. We celebrate important events in our lives with sexual intercourse.

There is nothing like celebrating being pregnant with having sex. We learned quickly that sex can relieve the tensions of jobs and even the occasional difficulties of raising teenage children. Sexual intercourse can be very helpful in healing hurts. We sometimes have sex before we discuss a tense issue. That puts the focus on us and not merely being right in the argument. At other times we finish the discussion by crawling into bed together and loving each other. One of our children is a result of this.

Children have a way of changing the lives of married couples, especially their physical relationship. It wasn't that we didn't have sex or that it was any less fulfilling, it just became more difficult to juggle our time schedules with babies that wake up at any time, the demands of jobs, taking care of a house, and being active in our church community. So as the years of having children passed, we settled into a routine. I knew that Bob wanted to have sex more frequently than we did. I teasingly referred to him as "Mr. Eveready." In reality we didn't go for long periods of time without sex. "Quickies" were often all the time we had or needed, but it kept us physically close to each other. Sometimes I found the energy demanded by small children left me uninterested by the end of the day and longed for time to just be alone with Bob without sexual intimacy. I knew that he was sometimes frustrated, but I didn't see us as any different from other married couples after hearing them talk at social gatherings. We did find ways and times to keep sex in our lives and I was energized after we made love. We even managed some incredibly wonderful evenings, mornings or afternoons together.

I have come to realize that one of the best things I did for our sexual relationship was to become comfortable with the body that God has given me. When we were married I was very, very thin. My brothers used to joke that if I stood sideways and stuck out my tongue, I'd look like a zipper, or if I drank tomato juice, I'd be a thermometer. Added to that, Bob said on more than one occasion that one of the things he finds most attractive about me is my intellect. Over the years my body has changed and I have managed to stay relatively slender, but accepting my body has been a long process. Presenters at a workshop once said it is a good thing that breasts come in two's. Women believe that theirs are too big, too small, too far apart or too close together, too high up or too down low. Even more so, every woman is convinced that there is a perfect pair and she doesn't have them. My body may not be perfect but it is what I have. There are some things about my body that I can control. I worked hard to get back in shape after each pregnancy. Several years ago I decided that I wasn't taking very good care of my body. I want to be able to continue to travel well into old age and maintain utmost mobility as well. I told Bob I was going to start an exercise routine and he joined me. It has had a double effect. I am more physically fit and we have time together most days. Besides, his discipline keeps me going with the exercise routine when I don't want to exercise.

I figured out that it is important for me to look nice for Bob. I know I dress up to impress others when we go out for the evening or each day when I go to work, so why not for Bob as well. It wasn't that he didn't love me in nursing bras and sweats, but keeping that physical attraction there was also important. After all, dressing well was one of the things that attracted us to each other. So, I have bought sexy nightgowns to wear not just on special occasions, and reasonably nice things to wear on weekends when we are out and about. Bob has done the same. I like seeing his cute little buns in sexy black briefs rather than his usual "tidy whities" or in silky boxers rather than utilitarian ones. Besides, it is fun to buy them for him as various holidays approach. All of this has helped me to believe that in spite of the passing years, I still am attractive to him.

One of the best things for our sexual relationship is change. While our making love has some aspects of being routine, like having sex nearly every Saturday morning, we still try new things. Periodically we buy books on sexual techniques and read them together or we watch a sexy movie together. On a rainy day, when we were on vacation, we went to a bath and body products' store. We smelled every scent until we found the one that was sensual for both of us. Half the fun was watching the people in the store watching the middle age couple and seeing their faces as we brought our things to be checked out. Then we went back to the condo and gave each other a massage. Our culture tells us that when the excitement of the honeymoon wears off, we should find a new partner. We say change, but make it in your sexual activities. We can change the where, the when, and the how. The location in our house is important to us. We have made love by the fire, by candlelight in our bedroom, on the deck at our campground (that took a lot of convincing on Bob's part) or in a hotel for the weekend. In a discussion with other couples, we discovered that we were the only ones who had not had sex in the backseat of a car. That has been added to the things that we haven't tried yet. As our schedules have changed along with our bodies, we find mornings more fulfilling for us. What we do and the changes we make are part of our journey. A candlelight bubble bath in our whirlpool tub is wonderful place to start, as is the touching and talking in the car on the way home from a meeting or work.

Once in a while things we try bring different results than expected. After being introduced to the idea of giving each other a massage and buying some wonderfully scented almond massage cream, we used it one evening. One of our children crawled into bed with us the next morning, began to sniff at the air, put his/her nose under the sheets and came out saying, "There has to be chocolate chip cookies in here somewhere." We still find the scent of almonds very sensual, but frequently laugh about chocolate chip cookies.

One of the advantages of having friends who are also working on their sexual relationship is that we share and pick up ideas from each other (in conversations, not activities). Of the many things that other couples said they tried, we found that some were merely okay, some wonderful like an evening at a hotel which caters to the every desire of a couple, and some we merely agreed were not for us (mirrors on the ceiling). One of the things that Bob suggested in jest was to have sex standing up in a hammock. Perhaps it's just his ultimate fantasy. We know a couple who tried it and say it can't be done. It took some fast thinking to explain to our children why a hammock had been tied between the trees in our backyard by our friends one evening.

We live in a world where touching is usually for the young. My students seem to need a few seconds more of physical contact as the bell rings before they go into separate classes. Yet adults quickly give up physical contact. When we dated, cars had bench seats. I sat in the middle so it was easy (and probably dangerous) for Bob to put his arm around me as he drove, to hold hands, or to steal a kiss at the stoplight. Like others, after we married, I moved to the passenger side of the car. Maintaining physical contact is very important to us.

It is not uncommon for us to hold hands under the table at a restaurant when we are out with friends. Even with bucket seats we hold hands often as we drive. Bob spends a lot of time at a computer and I can massage his shoulders or kiss the balding spot on his head and then leave the room. Of course Bob has to have his little squeeze on his favorite part of my body at least twice a day.

Another dimension of touching is "skin-to-skin," being naked with each other and feeling every part of each other's body without the expectation of sexual intercourse. To get us used to this, each evening when we went to bed we took off all our clothes and just lay next to each other or in each other's arms and allowed ourselves to touch and be touched. It resulted in great closeness. Sometimes it led to sex but that was never our intention. We talked as we touched each other, usually not about sex. It was soothing to be in contact as we discussed our day or plans for the upcoming weekend. We talked about where we liked to be touched and where we didn't. I had a lot of fun discovering and talking about where Bob is ticklish. This is a wonderful way to love each other when sexual intercourse isn't possible or wanted.

I found this very freeing. Bob caressing my body didn't always mean that he wanted to have sex. Many times he just liked to feel my body. It took me a while to get comfortable with this. He frequently came up behind me as I was preparing dinner. He always kissed me but sometimes the lingering or additional touches left me wondering what he expected. Now I enjoy the moment and then say, "Are you asking?" He'll say, "Yes" or "No," depending on the situation

and his feelings. This helps me enjoy little moments of closeness that I might otherwise miss.

It will be interesting to see where the advancing years
take us. I'm sure it will be another part of the journey, with
more fun and adventure and perhaps a little misadventure
along the way.

Hints, Tips and Things We Learned Along the Way

* Enthusiastic couples often try to do every-thing at once. Remember that you have the rest of your life to work on your sexual rela-tionship. We suggest that you make a mutual decision about one or two things you would like to work on for a while. When you think you have made some progress, try something different.

* Trying new things must involve mutual con-sent. Surprise does have its place but most major changes require a discussion first. Make sure that your fantasies are agreeable to your spouse. A friend was traveling and bought his wife a sexy black teddy in anticipation of his return home and making love to her. When he gave it to her he was surprised and hurt by her response that she would never wear that "thing."

* Child swapping, - not spouse swapping. Among your closest and trusted friends, do children swapping occasionally. You keep their kids one night and then they keep yours. Plan a romantic evening together without the kids.

* Be creative in the things you try. The pos-sibilities are endless.

1. One Halloween a friend went out the back door in just her long coat, rang the front door bell and said, "Trick or treat!" and flashed her husband as he stood there with the basket of candy. They both said that the treat that followed was worth the trick.

2. Another friend, whose children were away for the evening, went out for a leisurely dinner with her husband. As they finished placing their order she announced to her husband, "You know I have nothing on under this dress." He couldn't keep his hands off her under the table and she says it was the fastest dinner they ever ate.

3. A husband planned a wonderful evening for his wife. He arranged for his mother to keep the kids overnight. When his wife came home from work, a sign on the entry door told her to go to their bathroom. There she found a candlelit room with a hot bath drawn complete with floating rose petals and candles. On the towel she found a note that said a limousine would pick her up in an hour and she didn't need to bring anything with her. The limousine took her to an expensive hotel where he met her for a candlelight dinner and more.

4. Then there is the friend who knows that it's all about timing. His wife is most responsive

sexually with a glass and a half of wine, not two glasses, but a glass and a half. So, he always watches carefully and quickly escorts her to the bedroom as she nears the half glass mark on her second glass.

❋ There are many "how to" books on the market. Find a book that you think will work for the two of you. A date to select the book is fun. Then crawl into bed and take turns reading sections or chapters of the book aloud to each other. Stop to take time to discuss and/or practice what you've read.

❋ As with all things in our lives, sexual activity may change with time but doesn't need to end. As your bodies age, medical help may be required. You might also check the bookstore for books which are specifically aimed at that time in your life.

❋ When we are considering trying something new, we use the following questions to help us decide what we will try or evaluate what we have tried.

1. How do I feel about myself doing this?
2. How do I feel about my partner doing this together?
3. How do I feel about the activity itself?
4. How do I feel about my relationship with God when we do this?

If we can comfortably answer all of these questions positively, it is likely something we would try or do again.

Questions to Help Guide Your Discussion/ Dialogue

Remember to share your feelings.

1. Where did I find me/us in Bob and Rita's story?

2. What attitudes do I bring to our sexual relationship?

3. How important do I think sex is to our relationship?

4. What do I like best about our sexual relationship?

5. What do I like least about our sexual relationship?

6. What do I like most about my body?

7. What do I like least about my body?

8. What do I like most about your body?

9. What do I like least about your body?

10. What makes it easy (difficult) for me to discuss this area of our relationship? (two questions)

11. Describe a time when our sexual activity made me feel especially close and intimate.

12. What changes do I think I could make in this area of our relationship? (This is recognition and possibly a commitment to change.)

REACHING OUT

"Lovebird 1 and Lovebird 2" — Bob

"…wanted a 'Mr. Boeke'…" — Rita

Bob

My family has a long history of involvement in the lives of others. My great-great grandmother left writings that made it clear that she and her husband had a great love for each other and that it empowered her. She was a midwife and counselor for the women in the pioneer settlement in which they lived. They adopted an orphan who became a priest and bishop. Sometimes she wrote the homily for the traveling priest when he visited their settlement. Boeke men seem to choose strong women to marry.

My parents often served the community through the Church and in other ways. For many years, my father was a township trustee. They were involved with extended family and neighbors, as well as raising their twelve children. They were always quick to respond to someone in need. As a result, it seemed natural to me that our marriage needed to go beyond the two of us and even beyond our children. Rita and I agreed while we were dating that we would serve the Church and others. It was only a question of what we would choose and when.

Early in our marriage, we became involved in discussion groups, helped with liturgy planning in our parish and taught religion to high school students. I think we were somewhat unusual in that we did these things together. Priests and other people we worked with seemed to like working with a married couple.

When we became involved in Marriage Encounter, we were expected to do everything together and we liked that. Couples on the retreats and workshops we gave seemed to find our story relatable and encouraged us to keep going or to "write a book." They told us stories of their lives that inspired us to work harder. We were very fortunate to be able to affect others in such positive ways.

While we spent a lot of time working specifically with couples, I discovered that our marriage had an effect on people in many cases when they only dealt with me and sometimes didn't even know Rita. One day a colleague came into my office and asked if he could talk to me. He was planning to be married and during the process, he and his fiancé had discovered that some of the differences in their backgrounds were more important than they thought. He was looking for advice from me about how to handle the situation. I was able to help him think through the ways that their differences would affect their lives together. As a result, they decided not to get married.

Two secretaries at work - one divorced, the other widowed – often liked to chat with me and frequently shared with me how their lives were going. Sometimes they looked for comfort or help. I was always surprised by their openness with me and was happy that my life with Rita helped me to know how to respond to them. Perhaps they found me a "safe" male to talk to because they knew the strength of my relationship with Rita.

When Rita went back to work, her primary ministry became her students and we dropped Marriage Encounter and most of our other commitments. That left me with a void in my life. At first I focused on my writing. My monthly columns were published in our parish bulletin and our diocesan newspaper. While I did the writing, most of the time I discussed my topics with Rita and let her review them before I sent them off for publication. Some of what I wrote focused on relationship issues. I liked writing, but it wasn't enough, so I told God to let me know when he wanted me to do something else.

Eventually I was drawn to the parish program of initiation of adults into the Church (RCIA). I was a sponsor for candidates and participated in presentations and discussions on a variety of topics. I found that it helped my presentations and participation in discussions when I shared some of our story in the process. Sometimes I would bring Rita with me to share a presentation. Later I became involved on a team for Landings, a process of welcoming Catholics back into the Church after they have been away. Part of the process included participants and team members telling their faith journey. I found that my journey could not be told without including Rita. When the program finished, the group was eager to meet her.

I spent a lot of my first year teaching in the high school learning to deal with high school students again. The first day of class one of my students came into the classroom, looked at me, and said, "Are you the teacher?" I responded that yes I was. She said again, "Are you really the teacher?" Then I caught on that she was expecting Rita. I quickly explained that I was Mr. Boeke. Since Rita and I both taught the same course for seniors, students would compare notes and sometimes try to get one of us to give them a break on an assignment by claiming that the other already had. They learned that we, too, compared notes and that they could not get between us.

When we were both on the team for a retreat the students heard each of us talk about the other. At the end of my presentation, Rita came up to give me a big kiss. I did the same after hers. Each time the students went wild applauding us. By the end of the retreat, they referred to us as Lovebird 1 and Lovebird 2. It was clear that they found our relationship to be very desirable and many of them talked about how they wanted a marriage like ours.

One day as we were getting into our car after school, a faculty member came up to us and told us that they heard a rumor that we had been seen holding hands in the hall. That apparently bothered somebody, but we thought it amusing. We have always kissed each other when we part. At school we never quite figured out whether we were saying goodbye when we separated to go to our own classrooms. We fell into a pattern of a quick kiss outside my classroom each morning. Students weren't quite sure what to make of that, but once they realized we are married, they liked it. We think it showed them that romance can survive no matter how long you are married.

Various comments we have heard indicate that many people in the school are aware of us, not just as two teachers, but as a couple. We don't know what it is that makes people pleasantly conscious of us or any other couple, but we suspect that it has something to do with our enthusiasm for each other and our exuberance about being married after forty years. We strongly believe that letting the world know of our joy in and enthusiasm for each other is a gift to all who meet us.

We both expect to end our formal teaching careers in a few years. We don't expect that doing so will end our opportunities to share our marriage with others. We have started to offer workshops for married couples and are considering offering workshops for high school students, but we are open to other options that we can't foresee. Maybe we will just be that old married couple that lives in our neighborhood. Yeah, right!

Rita

The second year I taught I was asked to teach a marriage course. Being married only a year, I had no idea what to do so I just began to share our life together with the girls in my class. I told them about the three promises we had made to each other on our honeymoon: to not let a day go by without verbally saying I love you, to never be apart without kissing each other goodbye and to fall asleep holding hands. Twenty years later at a school anniversary celebration, a student from that class came bounding across the room saying, "Mrs. Boeke, thank you for the advice. I've been married for ten years and my husband and I hold hands every night as we fall asleep. We tell everyone that we know who is getting married to do the same thing." I continue to tell this to my classes and on retreats. When a friend was getting married, she told everyone at her bridal shower what she heard me say on retreats. Then she proceeded to say that she and her husband were going to do the same thing. Marriages do have a way of touching others.

The friends we had when we were first married were the other young teachers with whom I taught. Being a newlywed, I told them I wanted to spend time with Bob when they invited me to join them after school. Very quickly they began to include Bob in whatever we were doing. Whether it was going out for a drink on Friday after school or weekend outings, they always thought of the "Boekes," not merely Rita joining them. They became our friends, not just mine. We were thought of as a couple, not only as an individual. When Bob started to work with me, we quickly became the "Boekes" to both adults and students. We had our own teaching styles and friends, but there was a dimension of the unity in our relationship that others expected.

My parents taught me the value of serving others. We fell into the same habit. At first it was the two elderly ladies who lived in our first apartment building, then the elderly couple that rented out the upstairs apartment of their home to us and eventually the couple who lived across the street. Whatever they needed us to do, we did. Sometimes it was just listening to them when they were lonely or doing odd jobs for them. Each of them always referred to us in some way as "the cute little couple." We went to Church regularly and while we weren't involved at first, our regular attendance and stopping to chat with the priests got us recognition. We were asked to get involved and invariably the person in charge commented about how much we loved each other. I didn't think we did anything out of the ordinary, but something in our actions seemed to attract attention to our couple relationship. Mostly it was our ease with each other and the comfort we had with being together, no matter what the activity.

Someone once told us that sex is intimate but not private. What they were conveying is that the behaviors we engage in with each other are intimate, but the fact that we have and enjoy a sexual relationship is not private. We have not hidden that from our children - even though they still squirm when we talk about it in front of them - and my students are aware as well. It has helped them to have positive attitudes about their own sexual behaviors and to counter what the media tells them. I think the same is true of marriage. Much of how we live is intimate, but not private. It needs to be shared with others. It brings hope to the world.

Having been given the opportunity to share our relationship with thousands of couples and numerous priests and bishops in our time of involvement in the Marriage Encounter movement makes us extremely fortunate. We touched people's lives and, on numerous occasions, received notes and phone calls thanking us for what we had done. Occasionally a couple has said, "You probably don't remember us but..." and they would continue to tell us how something we said in a talk or had written had helped them in their marriage. Talking about having sex in our closet brought a humorous response and we laughed with a couple when a husband told us he was mentally measuring their closet. We formed many friendships as a result of our involvement and our children's lives were enriched as well.

While being involved in Marriage Encounter allowed us to do "big" things, I think the "little" things we do touch just as many people's lives. We introduced ourselves to a couple at Church, become friends, and supported them through an annulment process. We had the privilege of witnessing their marriage when it was blessed in the Church. We knew we impacted others when we arrived at meetings and were referred to as the matched pair. Since Bob and I have been on our exercise routine, various young couples in our neighborhood tell us that we are their heroes and they want to be like us when they are our age. One couple is our next door neighbor but the other one we don't know very well. The wife is often outside with her children as we walk and she talks to us. Occasionally her husband joins her as well.

Since there wasn't enough time to do everything for school and be gone weekends, we slowed the intensity of our outside involvements when I went back to work. I realize today I didn't give up anything in that process. Teaching religion was a new opportunity God gave me and us to share our marriage with others. I found it very easy to speak about Bob when appropriate in my lesson for the day. I merely mentioned Bob in the prayer before class or told my students that we had talked about the topic the night before. It didn't matter what topic, it just seemed natural to mention him in some way. He often came along to my chaperoning responsibilities. Very quickly, girls began to say they wanted a "Mr. Boeke" when they got married. The first two schools at which I taught were schools for girls. I now teach at a co-ed school. The girls still continue to say the same thing, but what amazes me is when boys come to talk about their futures. They tell me that they want a marriage like ours and want to treat their wives the way they hear Bob treats me. Before he taught with me, students couldn't wait to meet him and have him come to the class to tell his side of the story. When he taught with me, they referred to us as "the Boekes" and compared over their lunches and on weekends what we had said about each other in class.

Hints, Tips and Things We Learned Along the Way

* To be its best, a marriage has to go beyond the two of you.

* The people who most need to experience your love are your children.

* If you are enthusiastic about your marriage, it will have a positive impact on others no matter what you do.

* Don't participate in gripe sessions about spouses. Try to sneak in a positive comment about each other instead.

* There are a myriad of ways to share your love for each other. It can be in Church, civic or community activities, but most often in ordinary things you do each day at work or in your neighborhood.

* The world needs to see that couples can love each other for a lifetime. How much you earn and what you do is less important than letting others see your love.

* Sometimes it is awkward or difficult to have the courage to share your relationship with others, but it is never without rewards.

Questions to Help Guide Your Discussion/Dialogue

Remember to share your feelings.

1. Where did I find me/us in Bob and Rita's story?

2. How do our children experience our love for each other?

3. Describe a time when I knew others were aware of our love.

4. Do I make use of opportunities to share our marriage with others?

5. How important do I think it is for us to make our marriage visible?

6. How do I think we might most effectively share our marriage relationship with others?

7. What rewards have I seen when we have shared our relationship?

8. What makes it easy/difficult for me to share our marriage?

THE POWER OF LOVE

"….level of delight…" — Bob

"…walk barefoot forever…" — Rita

Bob

When I was in high school and college and through the early years of our marriage, I appeared to others to be self-assured and confident – some have even said conceited. While that was the surface appearance, it was largely a front. I was confident of my intellectual ability but I wasn't very sure of myself in dealing with people. I was often aggressive in discussions and used my ability to speak well to prove my capabilities and worth to people. I was good at solving problems and sometimes tried to solve problems for people when they weren't even interested. I thought that people only liked the things I did for them but did not like me. It was difficult for me to carry on a polite conversation with someone I didn't know.

I found that Rita accepted me and liked me just as I was. I didn't have to worry about impressing her. Her unconditional love has continued through our lives together and the effect has been a total transformation for me. When we were dating and first married, she would sometimes snuggle up to me when we were dancing, put her head on my shoulder and look up at me with a look that melted me inside. It told me I was special and very much loved. She still looks at me that way occasionally. It keeps me alive and feeling loved for a long time each time I see it.

Rita's unconditional love for me has allowed me to be more open with her and with others. I have shared with her my greatest fears about myself, my secret dreams and my physical needs and have received only love in return. She gives me the courage to write a controversial column without fear about readers' reactions and take the risk of sharing with you private details of our lives together.

In my effort to love Rita and in being loved by her I have come to understand the meaning of the words in our wedding ceremony, "sacrifice may be difficult and irksome, love makes it easy and true love makes it a joy." Because of Rita's love, my ability to love has grown and I find it much easier to give to others and to find real joy in doing so. I am a more compassionate person. My first impulse is always to follow the rules and make people face the consequences of their actions. Compassion affected the way I dealt with our children as they grew up and affected my attitude toward my students. From Rita I learned the value of showing my care for them, even when I wasn't willing to give them all they wanted. I have become more willing to give someone a break or a second chance. I have learned to hold Rita, a child or a friend who is hurting and let them know I care without having to solve their "problem."

Rita's total love has convinced me that I am a lovable person and that others also like me for who I am. The self-confidence I gain from this is the most freeing thing that has ever happened to me. It gives me the confidence to approach a stranger at a party and introduce myself without fear of being rejected. It allows me to listen to others in a meeting without worrying that I haven't had a chance to speak, and it allows me to offer input with confidence when I do have something to add to the conversation.

This confidence helps me to enjoy our grown children and their spouses more. We have great discussions, and I have no hesitation in asking the kids for information or advice in their areas of expertise. I am pleased when they ask for my advice, but not upset if they don't take it.

It is Rita's trust in me that gave me the courage to apply for a high school teaching job at age 62, after several years of retirement. Her love gave me the confidence that I needed to work with high school students, something I thought that I would never do again. The warm reception I received from many faculty members reinforced my self-confidence.

The faith Rita has shared with me has also transformed me. When she went back to teaching and her classes were uncooperative, I was inspired by her reliance on prayer and God's help. It was amazing to see the results of her decision to love them. Praying with her has helped my faith to grow stronger and added to the presence of God in my life. I pray more and trust in God more than ever.

This sharing cannot be complete until I tell you about how Rita's love has raised the level of delight in my life. I am naturally a pretty happy and optimistic person. I get excited about ideas, so it is great to be able to share them with a person who also gets excited. She laughs at my wisecracks and sometimes blushes, but she can also answer with her own. I am delighted with our gentle teasing and feel wonderfully loved in it. I love her gentle touch. Her tender caring for my needs helps me to believe in myself.

I love to watch Rita doing many things. She reads to the grandkids and I just sit and watch. She has conversations with the kids and I'm happy to listen. I see her dealing with a problem at school, and I'm amazed at her people skills. Several times I have had one of her students or the parent of a student tell me how wonderful she is. They are always startled when I say, "I know! And I get to live with her!"

With the joy Rita's love brings to my life, everything is affected. I am delighted when a grandchild says, "Turn me upside down, Grandpa!" as she watches with a big smile on her face. Watching a rainbow, taking a picture of a wildflower, having a good day in class, and traveling anywhere is more fun because Rita is in my life. On a hard day she lifts my spirits. With Rita's love I see the world through a different lens. The colors I see are brighter, the power of thunderstorms more awesome, a day spent reading a book with her in the room more restful and a class taught well more rewarding. How wonderfully blessed I am!

Rita

Love changes everything. I'm not sure I can adequately describe for you all the changes that have happened. Nothing in my life is the same because I have tried to the best of my ability to totally love another person and be loved completely in return. I have been transformed in every aspect of who I am as a human being. I have been transformed intellectually, spiritually, emotionally and physically by Bob's love for me. While I am bound to Bob in a "forever" relationship, I am freer to be me in ways that I never dreamed could happen.

I have been challenged to grow intellectually by Bob's unending quest for knowledge. I have learned to believe more fully in my own innate abilities and have gained the confidence to be an active participant in the lively discussions and debates that we have. I can even lead the discussions and challenge him. It has helped me to use my leadership skills, and as a result, help my students learn to think critically as we study moral issues. It has given me the confidence to speak out when things aren't right and to acknowledge and apologize when I have made a mistake, not only with him, but with everyone who has been part of my life. He supported my decision to go back to work and to teach in a Catholic school even when we both knew it would affect our future financial security.

Physically I have been transformed as well. While those who knew me as I grew up can still recognize me, physically I am a different person. I would not describe myself as a physical risk taker. As a child it took a long time for me to decide to take physical risks. Learning to ride a bicycle was major, I never learned to roller skate and I avoided most amusement park rides. During our marriage I have tried things that as I child I would not have thought about doing. We have walked miles and miles throughout the world, and even taken a helicopter ride in South Africa, though I am afraid of heights. I have been through labor and delivery four times and would have willingly done it again if we'd had another child. Bob gave me physical freedom when he taught me to drive and I have driven the interstates and expressways in many major U. S. states and cities. On the other hand, his love has helped me acknowledge my limitations and he accepts it when I tell him I can't do something. He likes being adventuresome, especially when he can share it with me. He includes me in his new adventures and yet still gives me the confidence to bail out at the last minute when I don't think I can do it, whether it's handling the traffic in a construction zone, we are in the line for a roller coaster ride, or climbing steps to reach the top of a lighthouse. He has encouraged me to learn to swim and respects my lack of confidence when I am in the water. He has challenged me to try things in our sexual relationship and we have had wonderful experiences as a result. Yet he never demands that I give more than I'm comfortable doing. I'm convinced his love for me will help me to accept physical limitations that may arise as I continue to age.

I have been transformed emotionally as well. I always knew I had feelings. I grew up in a family where both men and women expressed their emotions. For the most part I felt free to laugh or cry or to be happy or sad. Bob's love for me has helped me to discover a depth to my emotions and to more fully express them. Thus I am a healthier person. There is nothing like the emotional fulfillment that comes after he has loved me and tended to my needs as well as his. It still amazes me what physical intimacy can do for my emotional well being. His love has awakened in me a depth of emotional responsiveness that I didn't know I had. He has helped me to see that it is okay to be angry with injustice, whether it was done against me or people I love. I have uncovered the depth of the gift of compassion that I have and yet have learned to stand up for my own rights. He has helped me to discover my instincts and know that if I listened to them they are most often correct when I am dealing with people and situations. I have laughed harder with him, sometimes so hard that I cry, and he has held me in his arms as I sobbed when I was overwrought with sadness, hurt or grief. He has gotten me to believe that it is okay to pamper myself, though I try to live a life of helping others. His love has helped me to experience being whole again emotionally when I didn't think I ever would.

Finally, I have been transformed spiritually in all the various aspects that the word conveys. Bob has helped me to discover, accept and enhance all the gifts that I have in being a woman and to recognize that it is okay to have strength as well as gentleness. He has helped me to see that it is okay to be assertive and not always assume the passive role. By his love for me, I have gained the confidence to accept myself as a leader while remaining compassionate. It has helped me to see myself as a more complete person. Every aspect of who I am, whether it is wife, daughter, mother, grandmother, sister, teacher, colleague or friend, has been permanently changed for the better. If that is not enough as I have learned to love him and be loved by him, I have experienced God more deeply than I ever thought I would. It has changed the way I pray, how I try to listen for direction in my life, and how I express my faith. As I have experienced his total commitment to me, it has strengthened my understanding of trust and I am able to see and live that in my relationship with God. For that I will forever be grateful. I would easily give up all the material possessions I have and walk barefoot forever if that meant I could have just one more day to love and be loved by him.

Questions to Help Guide Your Discussion/Dialogue

Remember to share your feelings.

1. Where do I find me/us in Bob and Rita's story?

2. How have I changed because you have loved me?

3. How have I changed because I have loved you?

4. How would I write our power of love story?

5. How would I want to spend "the day" in our 'Forever and a Day" together?

AFTERWORD

We thank you for taking the time to read our story of love, commitment, growth and trust. We hope you enjoyed it. While we knew we had lived a wonderful life together, we had no idea what the process of reflecting on our life and committing it to print would be. We laughed and cried together as we recalled the events that we shared with you. We frequently stopped to celebrate, savor and cherish our relationship. The process has challenged us and encouraged us to continue to live our forever commitment with each other. We hope you can use our story to help uncover, enhance and live, Forever and a Day, a great love story of your own.

ABOUT THE AUTHORS

Bob and Rita Boeke have presented hundreds of retreats, workshops and days of enrichment for married couples and priests since 1974. They have been featured speakers at regional and national conventions and have held leadership positions at the local, regional and national levels of Worldwide Marriage Encounter.

The Boekes present the **Forever and a Day** workshop for married couples, based on this book.

Bob & Rita's church activities include chairing liturgy and family life committees. They have designed and led marriage preparation programs and frequently speak to RCIA, high school groups and others about marriage. They have worked with the Office of Marriage and Family Life of the Archdiocese of Chicago to plan and promote programs and days of enrichment for married couples.

Bob has been a college professor and high school teacher of physics, mathematics and religion for more than thirty five years. He has presented teen retreats. His column on religion from a lay person's perspective has appeared in the **Catholic New World** and parish bulletins.

With nearly twenty five years of experience, Rita is a high school history and religion teacher specializing in scripture and morality. As a religion department chair and campus minister in Catholic high schools she has directed liturgy planning and teen retreats.

Bob and Rita have been married for more than forty years. They have four children and six grandchildren. They make their home in suburban Chicago.

FOREVER AND A DAY

A Time to Remember
Celebrate, and Believe
In the Power of Your Marital Love

A Workshop
by
Robert and Rita Boeke

For more information
or to schedule
Forever and a Day
Contact Bob & Rita Boeke at

foreverandaday@foxvalley.net
or
readabookpress.com

Comments from Forever and a Day workshop attendees

"The workshop was definitely time well spent. Bob and Rita's 'from the heart' stories were relatable and inspiring. We discovered new insights and ways to strengthen our love"

Jim and Marie Lynch
Marriage Encounter Presenters

"Bob and Rita Boeke have the rare gift of sharing their lived experiences in a unique and easy manner that challenges others to experience the mystery of the human body and God. Their presentations challenge married couples to share the joys and sorrows, highs and lows of daily living."

Fr. Mel Hemann
Marriage Retorno

It was an "awesome" day! Your enthusiasm and support inspired us and the other couples attending.

John and Marcia Seiler

We talked about issues we had never discussed before and are moving forward to discuss more.

Couple married more than 20 years

Good topics, concise presentations with humor to make us "laugh" at our own mistakes.

Workshop attendee

3921777